A History of Florida through New World Maps

Borders of Paradise

Edited by Dana Ste.Claire

With catalogue annotations and essay by Peter A. Cowdrey, Jr.
and essays by Dana Ste.Claire

University Press of Florida

Gainesville ‖ Tallahassee ‖ Tampa ‖ Boca Raton
Pensacola ‖ Orlando ‖ Miami ‖ Jacksonville

02 01 00 99 98 97 6 5 4 3 2 1

Library of Congress Cataloging-in-Publication Data

Borders of paradise.
    A history of Florida through New World maps: borders of paradise
    edited by Dana Ste.Claire: with catalogue annotations and essay
by Peter A. Cowdrey, Jr., and essays by Dana Ste.Claire.
        p.   cm.
    Originally published: Borders of paradise. Daytona, Fla.: Museum
of Arts and Sciences, 1995.
    Includes bibliographical references (p.   ).
    ISBN 0-8130-1511-1 (alk. paper)
    1. Florida—Maps—Early works to 1800.   I. Ste.Claire, Dana.
II. Cowdrey, Peter A.
    GA 418.B67   1997
    912.759—dc20   96-43617

Editor: Dana Ste.Claire
Book Design: Cohn Barnes
Photography: James Quine
Production: Stacey Stivers

On the Cover: Detail, MAP OF LA FLORIDA, c. 1584, hand-colored engraving by Abraham Ortelius.

Back Cover: VIEW OF ST. AUGUSTINE HARBOUR, c. 1671, hand-colored engraving by Arnoldus Montanus.

SANDRA B. MORTHAM, SECRETARY OF STATE

A History of Florida through New World Maps: Borders of Paradise is funded in part by the Bureau of Historical Museums, Division of Historical Resources, Florida Department of State, and Rand McNally.

The University Press of Florida is the scholarly publishing agency for the State University System of Florida, comprised of Florida A & M University, Florida Atlantic University, Florida International University, Florida State University, University of Central Florida, University of Florida, University of North Florida, University of South Florida, and University of West Florida.

University Press of Florida
15 Northwest 15th Street
Gainesville, FL 32611

TABLE OF CONTENTS

PREFACE

From a time before John Bartram published his famous *Travels* in 1791, the state of Florida has enjoyed an emerging and developing geographic identity based on information gathered by hosts of explorers who visited and charted this "frontier Eden." As early as the end of the 15th century, with the travels of both Cabot and Vespucci, explorers and adventurers attempted to map this New World. Ponce de Leon, Hernando de Soto and Jean Ribault all contributed to an enlightened vision of Florida in the 16th century, captured and expressed by a host of European mapmakers. But it was probably the 1763 transfer of Florida from Spain to England that drove the need for more accurate and precise boundaries to this tropical paradise. And, with statehood in 1845, the legal description of the state was finally established.

It is a great pleasure for The Museum of Arts and Sciences to work with donors Kenneth Worcester Dow and Marc Davidson, scholars Peter A. Cowdrey Jr. and Dana Ste.Claire to produce *A History of Florida through New World Maps*, a glimpse into the important cartographic record of Florida. Special thanks are extended to Secretary of State Sandra B. Mortham, the Division of Historical Resources, and the 1995 Historic Preservation Advisory Council: Augusta Bird, Frances F. Bourque, Jean H. Bunch, Arnold Greenfield, Alvin B. Jackson, Jr., Janet Synder Matthews, Raphael Penalver, Sylvia Vega Smith, Dana Ste.Claire, Doris Tillman, Antonia F. Vogt, Laura C. Ward and George Percy, Director of the Division of Historical Resources, for their continuing support of Florida history projects. Final thanks are extended to the Board of Trustees of The Museum of Arts and Sciences: Dr. Roger Lewis, President; Stuart Sixma, Past President; CiCi Brown, Vice President; Thomas Hart, Vice President; Antoinette Slick, Vice President; Blaine Lansberry, Secretary; Marc Davidson, Assistant Secretary; Olga Gomon, Treasurer; John E. Graham Jr., Assistant Treasurer; Brop Kelly Burnett, Representative to Executive Board; Betty Bivings, Lonnie Brown, Linda Carley, Sheila Crawford, Pramila Desai, Marilyn Chandler Ford, A. Brooks Harlow Jr., Cheryl Lentz, Jamie Moore, David Neubauer, Susan Root, David Sacks, Walter W. Snell, D. Glenn Vincent, Allison Zacharias; Janice Griffin, Guild President; Lydia Simko, Guild Vice President; Dorothy Bradley, Guild Representative; Deborah B. Allen and Rosaria Upchurch, Junior League of Daytona Beach Co-Presidents; Dr. Inez Marchand, Junior League Vice President; and Edith Lamb and Julian Lopez, Cuban Foundation Representatives, for their continued commitment to Florida history.

GARY R. LIBBY

DIRECTOR

THE MUSEUM OF ARTS AND SCIENCES

View of St. Augustine Harbour with the Castillo de San Marcos fortress and exaggerated topography, including mountains, in background. *Pagus Hispanorum in Florida*, by Arnoldus Montanus c. 1671, Amsterdam. Hand-colored wood engraving, gift of Kenneth Worcester Dow and Mary Mohan Dow, 91.01.528.

Borders of Paradise

Florida is an immense land, bounded by three rivers, one long ocean shoreline, and two imaginary lines. The strangely configured state measures 447 miles north to south from the St. Marys River to Key West, and 361 miles east to west from the Atlantic Ocean to the Perdido River on the Alabama border, some 58,560 square miles in all. But the face of Florida as we know it today has changed dramatically since its European discovery by Juan Ponce de Leon in 1513. In three centuries and under four flags, Florida evolved geographically from the Spanish period La Florida, a sprawling uncharted territory comprised of all lands north and east of Mexico in North America, to a union state in 1845 with defined borders and definite identity.

Along the way, four powerful countries — Spain, France, Britain, and the United States — reshaped Florida, geographically, culturally and politically. These changes are reflected in the rich cartographic record of the state beginning nearly 500 years ago, when Florida became the first name of European origin to be etched upon New World maps. Following its discovery, the Florida territory served for centuries as a major mapping and navigational focal point for the Americas.

Florida has the longest recorded history of any of the American states in that it was the first to be discovered and occupied by Europeans. On the road to becoming a state, Florida was explored by Spanish conquistadors in an unyielding quest for fortune, then shaped by the Revolutionary War during the short-lived English occupation, and finally tamed as an unruly territory by the politics of union statehood. Each remarkable event contributed to what Florida is today — its people, its geography, and its identity as a place.

Historically a paradise to many and a problem for others, the story of Florida is a fascinating and lengthy tale of multiculturalism and determination. The rich and varied historical development of the Florida territory into an American state is a colorful compendium that can be read chapter by chapter through the rich repository of New World maps and drawings available to Florida history enthusiasts.

DANA STE.CLAIRE

A History of Paradise

Dana Ste.Claire

An Unbordered Paradise: Florida Before Conquest

By the time the Spanish arrived in the Americas in the 16th century, Florida had been occupied and settled for thousands of years by a widespread population of indigenous peoples. The rich environments of the region, mainly the vast coastal lagoons and enormous interior freshwater river basins, provided an abundance of food and other materials that attracted and sustained large groups of Native Americans for centuries.

The aboriginal societies that emerged from Florida were hardly the savages that historically have been portrayed for the New World. Although many of their customs were unusual in the eyes of Europeans, they were a highly sophisticated group of people who were well adapted to the challenging Florida environment. Long before Columbus landed, they had organized themselves into complex social systems in extensive villages and towns. Their political networks were intricate and far-reaching and their medical practices were equal or superior to any of those known in Europe at the time.

These first peoples of a boundless Florida paradise provided the foundation on which most European settlements in the region were built, many of which would later would become major cities and towns. Following contact by early explorers and colonists, the indigenous peoples of Florida became hosts to a growing population of foreigners and quickly had to adjust to a new way of life. In a short period of time, the natives were subjected to a variety of social and political pressures — they were introduced to new religions, often cruelly treated, and sometimes used as slaves.

Although many resisted the European intrusion, few natives could combat Old World sicknesses to which they had little or no resistance. The European settlers had unknowingly brought with them deadly diseases. Within two centuries following Ponce de Leon's discovery, thousands of aborigines in Florida and millions throughout the Americas died in epidemics. It was this devastating pestilence that led to the demise of a widespread and complex Native American culture in Florida.

The New World in the Eyes of Explorers

Ironically, it was the same Spanish conquest that displaced, both inadvertently and intentionally, New World indigenous cultures that provide us with the best ethnographic accounts of early Native Americans. These early descriptions and illustrations, jotted down by explorers, commissioned artists, mapmakers, and curious soldiers, provide us with an understanding of the lifestyles of the once-numerous original Americans.

Although relatively few in number, accurate portrayals of New World life occurred when artists began to accompany expeditions to the Americas in the 16th century. However, exaggerated depictions of the new continents continued and abounded during this time, feeding the appetites of Europeans hungry for fantasy accounts of lost paradises and evolving primitive worlds filled with savage races of cannibals and unusual animals like the alligator and the armadillo.

In many instances, Native Americans were represented in classical fashion, a contemporaneous European style. Artists favored heroic poses for the aborigines, nurturing the concept of the noble savage, another product of the European imagination. The second half of the 16th century saw an increasing tendency to romanticize the natives in classic style.

For some time, European images of the New World were created largely by artists who had never been there. It was common for 16th and 17th century European artists to borrow from and embellish works by artists such as Jacques le Moyne and John White who had made firsthand renderings of the new land. In turn, these highly stylized depictions were widely reproduced and circulated, rarely acknowledging the original artist. Through the early 19th century, these images, many of which appeared as engravings in literary works, helped to shape the Old World perspective of New World life.

As Florida was the first territory to be explored, many early New World images of America were taken from this region. Illustrations of Timucuan Indian life in northeastern Florida by Jacques le Moyne de Morgues are among the most important ethnographic depictions of Native Americans produced during the discovery period.

Le Moyne was the first trained artist to undertake a New World voyage specifically to illustrate scenes of America. He accompanied Rene de Laudonniere's expedition to Florida in 1564-65 that crossed the Atlantic to establish new French territories. Trained in the Gothic and Early Renaissance traditions, le Moyne's artistic depictions of the New World are particularly skillful. His portrayals of Timucuan Indian life in Florida remain as the primary reference source for historians and archaeologists

An early European image of Florida natives. *Floridaners of 1500*, by J. Trentsensky c. 1825, Wien, Austria; after Jacques le Moyne, c. 1564. Lithograph, gift of Kenneth Worcester Dow and Mary Mohan Dow, 91.01.574.

who study early Native American lifestyles in North America.

Unfortunately, all but one of le Moyne's original paintings depicting the New World have disappeared. His works are known mostly from engravings in *Brevis narratio,* a 13-volume compendium on America published in 1591 by Theodore de Bry. While le Moyne witnessed and documented many New World scenes, the majority of his works probably were done from memory rather than from life. Le Moyne's hasty departure from Florida with Laudonniere in 1565, fleeing a Spanish assault, may account for his abandoned field sketches. It is likely that he reconstructed his visual record of the New World during the voyage home, with final paintings completed in France and England.

Le Moyne's works were reproduced as engravings by de Bry, who following le Moyne's death in 1588, purchased the original paintings from his widow. De Bry in many cases added details to le Moyne's works that were not accurate New World portrayals. De Bry's engravings of le Moyne's works received wide circulation and thus accounted for much of the European perspective of the New World. In turn, these works were widely reproduced by hundreds of artists in the 17th and 18th centuries.

La Florida: The Spanish Claim

Following Christopher Columbus' first voyage to the Bahamas in 1492, a number of European expeditions were organized to explore and settle the New World. During a subsequent 25-year period, explorers moved north from the Caribbean region, contacting the southern peripheries of what is today the United States. By 1530, the coastal geography of Florida was known, as was most of the eastern seaboard of North America.

Early on, the Spanish, French, and English had interests in the New World territories. The French in 1564 were the first to seek control of the Florida territory, a wilderness Spain believed to be economically worthless. Subsequent 16th century expeditions by the French and English accelerated plans by Spain to colonize the Americas, particularly Florida, Europe's first frontier in North America. In 1565, Pedro Menendez de Aviles established the settlement of St. Augustine, today the oldest continuously occupied city in the United States. St. Augustine preceded by decades the English settlements of Jamestown, Virginia, in 1607 and Plymouth, Massachusetts, in 1620.

Fueled by gold, silver, precious gems, and a lucrative slave trade, Spain's empire flourished in the New World. By 1600, Spain's power over the southeastern region of North America was accepted throughout the world. The Spanish claim of New World lands, known as La Florida, encompassed lands north and east of Mexico. This seemingly boundless territory, stretching north from the Florida Keys to Newfoundland and west to Texas, would gradually diminish over the following two centuries due to English colonial encroachment.

Spain on the Halifax: New World Explorers in East Florida

Because of its close proximity to the Caribbean, peninsular Florida was the first region of mainland America to be "discovered" and explored. During the early 16th century, the east coast of Florida was quickly established as a major seaway channel for Spanish ships to sail into the Atlantic on their homeward journey. Hence, Spanish activity along the coastal regions of the state was once prevalent.

The most famous of New World explorers in Florida was the state's official discoverer, Juan Ponce de Leon, an experienced Spanish sailor who accompanied Columbus on his second voyage in 1493. Although there are hints of prior activity along Florida coasts — Spanish pirates and slavers surely had been there before — Juan Ponce generally is credited with finding Florida because his 1513 voyage was conducted under official Spanish auspices and documented in government records. In that he is credited as the first European to make contact with the continental mainland, Ponce de Leon, rather than Columbus, is arguably the real Old World discoverer of America proper.

While it generally is believed that Juan Ponce was in search of the fabled Fountain of Youth, it is doubtful if the legendary spring was a vital part of his quest. At the time, the myth was neither unique nor an important part of Spanish thinking on New World explorations. It is more probable that Juan Ponce's motivation was based in the wealth and power he thought he would achieve through his New World discoveries. Through a contract with the Spanish government, he had been promised a substantial share of all revenues from newly established territories.

Juan Ponce's historic voyage began in Puerto Rico, where he was serving as commander of a Spanish fort. From there he set sail in early March with three ships that he supplied with his own money, lured by uncharted and unexplored lands believed to be located to the north.

On April 2, 1513, Juan Ponce touched the Florida coast for the first time, thinking the new land was yet another island of the Caribbean. Landing somewhere near St. Augustine or, according to the most recent accounts, just south of Cape Canaveral, he took possession of the territory in the King's name and called it La Florida after Pascua Flores, the Feast of the Resurrection or Flowers, at Easter. It also has been chronicled that he named the land so because it appeared "delightful, having many pleasant groves."

Following this celebrated landfall, Juan Ponce sailed along the Gulf Stream where the strong Atlantic current swept away one of his ships, a

A 17th century view of the Spanish colonial city of St. Augustine. *Die Stadt Dels H. Augustins in Florida*, c. 1675, Germany. Engraving, gift of Kenneth Worcester Dow and Mary Mohan Dow, 94.01.580.

brigantine. Reorganizing, Juan Ponce anchored his two remaining ships off the coast of present-day New Smyrna Beach. Soon after, several Indians came down to the shoreline and began to hail the Spanish leader. As described by Antonio de Herrera in his *Decada Segunda*, an early history of Spanish colonization in the New World, what began as a peaceful excursion to the shore by Juan Ponce and his men turned into a minor skirmish with the Native Americans who attempted to take the Spanish boat:

"Here Juan Ponce went on shore, called by the Indians, who immediately tried to take the boat, the oars and arms. And not to break with them they suffered them, and in order not to alarm the land. But because they struck a seaman in the head with a stick, from which he remained unconscious, they had a fight with them who with their arrows and armed staves, the points of sharpened bones and fish spines, wounded two Spaniards, and the Indians received little harm. The night separated them, Juan Ponce regathered the Spaniards after hard work. He departed there to a river where he took water and firewood, and was awaiting the brigantine. Sixty Indians ran there to hinder him. He took one of them for a pilot, so that he might learn the language. He gave this river the name La Cruz (the Cross) and he left, in it, one of hewn stone with an inscription; they did not finish taking water because it was brackish."

The river named Rio de la Cruz or "River

An Old World view of New World peoples and their customs and houses. *Habits et Maison de Floridiens*, by Bernard c. 1700, France. Etching, gift of Kenneth Worcester Dow and Mary Mohan Dow, 91.01.459.

of the Cross" by Juan Ponce is noted by some historians as the body of water formed by the intersecting or crossing of Spruce Creek and the Halifax (or Indian) River near New Smyrna Beach. Today, this area is called Ponce de Leon Inlet.

Earlier this century, a group of historians proposed that New Smyrna was the original site of the early Spanish settlement of St. Augustine. The antiquities of New Smyrna, including a foundation that was thought to be an old Spanish fort and a sugar mill that resembles a Spanish mission, were thought to be the work of Menendez de Aviles in 1565. An early Spanish map dated 1601 shows St. Augustine located much farther south than where it stands today, but this is surely the result of exaggerated topography, a characteristic of early New World maps. While Menendez frequented the eastern coast of Florida, it is doubtful he is responsible for any construction in New Smyrna.

In 1605, Spanish explorer Alvaro Mexia traveled to and documented a number of Native American settlements along the east coast of Florida. He was sent to the territory by the government of Spain to investigate East Florida waterways, among other things. Perhaps the best known of Mexia's documented aboriginal sites is the town of Nocoroco at the northern tip of Tomoka State Park in Ormond Beach. This area was once the strategic location for a large group of Timucuan Indians and served as a political focal point for other groups living in the

Tomoka River Basin. Nocoroco is one of the latest Timucuan sites known in East Florida, having been occupied by Native Americans into the 18th century.

The explorer also described the activities at the Surruque at Turtle Mound of another group of Timucuans. The site, now part of Canaveral National Seashore, was a focal point for indigenous people in the area. In a report to Spanish Governor Pedro de Ybarra of St. Augustine, Mexia describes Baradero de Suroc, today known as Turtle Mound:

"The river pursues its way to the southeast, all through mangrove islands and sand mounds and palmetto groves and hillocks of low evergreen, oaks on its east bank. It makes many turns and twists, and passes the foot of a mound which they call the Mound of Surruque. This is a hill of oyster shell and short grass, and at the foot of the said hill the Indians of Surruque launch their canoes and go to sea."

Somewhere between Nocoroco at Tomoka and Turtle Mound, Mexia observed a huge Indian town called Caparaca. Once thought to be located near the present-day city of New Smyrna Beach, it is possible that it was farther north, as evidenced by recent archaeological investigations. More likely, the site of Caparaca is an extensive shell and sand burial mound complex located in the lower Spruce Creek basin.

Spanish activity along the east coast of Florida increased as Spain's empire strengthened, fueled by gold and silver from Central and South America. The Spanish began yearly treasure fleets in 1552 in an attempt to strengthen Spain's economy. The ships traveled from Colombia to Mexico; from there to Havana, Cuba, along the east coast of Florida, and finally homeward to Spain via Bermuda.

In the late 16th century, there were often 110 Spanish ships sailing in the fleet, but after a decrease in New World silver production and an increase in pirate attacks in the mid 17th century, only 17 ships sailed annually.

A powerful hurricane in 1715 sank 11 of 12 Spanish galleons off the east coast of Florida. The ill-fated treasure fleet was carrying an enormous amount of gold and silver bullion and coin, as well as a heavy cargo of amethyst and jewelry. Until 1719, the Spanish returned periodically to salvage the treasure. Still, a good amount of sunken treasure remains on the floor of the Atlantic. Today, archaeologists working with treasure salvors continue their search for undiscovered Spanish shipwrecks in an attempt to better understand early New World enterprises in La Florida.

The British Floridas

English colonists in pursuit of greater New World resources gradually pushed the northern borders of Spain's La Florida territory southward into present-day southern Georgia. The British finally took control of Florida in 1763 in exchange for the port city of Havana, Cuba, which had been captured by the English during the Seven Years' War (1756-63). The Spanish fled the province soon after Spain ceded it to the British, leaving Florida virtually empty.

The treaty with Spain further diminished the Florida territory, with the western boundary of Florida placed at the Mississippi River. The new borders included the early settlements of Mobile (Alabama), Baton Rouge (Louisiana), and Natchez (Mississippi). The Florida lands were so extensive from east to west that the British divided the province into two separate colonies, East Florida with St. Augustine as its capital and West Florida with its political seat at Pensacola. The two British Floridas, separated by the Apalachicola River near Tallahassee, became the 14th and 15th English colonies in North America.

The English had ambitious plans for the two Florida colonies. Settlers were attracted with offers of large land grants for the production of cotton, indigo, and other export crops, and the province of Florida once again was populated. The first major roadway in Florida, the Old

King's Road, was built to connect New Smyrna in the south with St. Marys on the Georgia border. But the British rule lasted only two decades, hardly enough time for the new English colonies to prosper. During this short occupation, however, the British were successful in mapping much of the interior Florida territory.

The most ambitious attempt by the British to colonize Florida took place at New Smyrna on the east coast. The account of this 18th century English settlement is an important but often forgotten chapter in the historical and cultural development of the state.

In 1767, Dr. Andrew Turnbull, a Scottish physician, and a group of British investors financed a settlement near the present-day city of New Smyrna Beach. Turnbull and his group had obtained from the British government a sizable land grant at New Smyrna to establish a large colony.

Early on, Turnbull sought out potential colonists from the Mediterranean because he believed people from these regions could better tolerate the Florida climate in that they were accustomed to working in warm temperatures. He recruited more than 1,000 natives of Minorca in the Baleric Islands to colonize his land. Along with the Minorcans, Turnbull gathered up Greeks, Italians and Corsicans for his experiment. New plans were drawn and seven more ships were acquired to accommodate a group three times larger than what was anticipated.

It took three months for the fleet to make its way to Florida. The ships arrived in St. Augustine in the summer of 1768, and several sailed from there down the coast to the newly established colony of New Smyrna, named for the birthplace of Turnbull's wife, whom he married in Smyrna, Asia Minor.

Unfortunately, preparations at the New Smyrna colony had been made for about 500, not the 1,255 who eventually arrived. Shortages of supplies and labor, and hard work in a hostile, mosquito-infested environment took their toll quickly. In less than a decade, the number of colonists dwindled to 600.

In 1777, the remaining settlers, most of whom were Minorcan, sought refuge in St. Augustine from the ill-fated colony. Governor Patrick Tonyn released them from their indentured service to Turnbull and settled them in the northern portion of the city, where many of their descendants live today.

Records will show that the greatest English attempt to settle Florida was in fact a Minorcan endeavor. Their influence, along with the contributions of Greeks and Italians from the same colony, provided the ethnic diversity for which early St. Augustine has been historically noted.

The American Revolution in Florida

July 4, 1776, was a busy day in the history of the United States. Delegates of the Second Continental Congress in Philadelphia adopted the Declaration of Independence, denouncing the tyrannical rule of King George III of England. The birth of a new republic was celebrated throughout the northern colonies.

Meanwhile in Florida, there were few observances of the historic occasion. Settlers carried on with life as normal in the two British Floridas, unaware of the turbulent uprisings to the north. When the news of the rebellion finally reached Florida on July 20 of that year, Floridians were outraged. Very few joined in the festivities, and those who did were quickly ridiculed. In fact, rioting against British authority in Florida was viewed as nothing less than treason.

Instead of celebrating, many Florida colonists denounced the challenge to British rule by burning effigies of John Hancock and Samuel Adams in the public square in St. Augustine and by drinking to the health and success of King George with great fervor.

Floridians were mostly Tories, very comfortable with the authority of the British Parliament and the political state of affairs. Overtaxation was never an issue in Florida because for years the territory had reaped the benefits of English taxes. Money raised by the Stamp Act and other types of taxation by the British government had been spent generously throughout the Floridas.

While the fires of independence were burning in Boston and Philadelphia, Florida remained loyal to the Crown. But it was not completely uninvolved in events surrounding the revolution. Paul Revere, known for his midnight ride in Boston, had just finished engraving the maps for Bernard Roman's *A Concise Natural History of East and West Florida*. Revere knew the geography of Florida well through his work.

In New Smyrna, the most ambitious attempt by the British to colonize Florida was failing in 1776. Andrew Turnbull's settlement was disbanding at New Smyrna as colonists made preparations to leave the ill-fated colony.

St. Augustine, capital of British East Florida. Steel engraving by English artist Harry Fenn, first published 1872. St. Augustine Historical Society collections.

more American in atmosphere as large numbers of settlers arrived from the northern states.

Weakened by the expansion of the newly formed United States of America, the second Spanish reign would be short lived. Spain's military was too small to defend its territory and under a growing threat of invasion, slowly relinquished its hold on Florida.

After several incursions into the territory by the American military, Spain ceded Florida to the United States in 1821. In exchange, America canceled Spain's debt of five million dollars. On July 10, 1821, in St. Augustine, the Spanish flag was lowered and the Stars and Stripes was raised for the first time in Florida. A similar event took place in Pensacola for West Floridians.

General Andrew Jackson was charged with establishing a new territorial government for the United States in Florida. Known for his relentless attacks on the Seminole Indians, Spanish settlers, and runaway slaves, Jackson was a hero to some, but a menace to many Floridians. Nevertheless, it was he who set into motion the process that would carry Florida from an unruly frontier territory to a union state.

While Jackson's stay was short — he left Florida three months after the American flag was first raised — his political actions were swift. He quickly merged the British-formed East and West Floridas into one territory, and formed two large counties, St. Johns and Escambia. Each county seat was provided with a mayor, a judge, and a court system.

Soon after Jackson's departure, William P. Duval was appointed by President James Monroe as the first territorial governor of Florida. One of Duval's most notable actions was to create a capital at Tallahassee, halfway between St. Augustine and Pensacola, the original governmen-

A Frontier Land

At the conclusion of the war for American independence, Spain, which participated in the American Revolution indirectly as an ally of France, regained the Florida province through the 1783 Treaty of Paris. Spain kept in place the British division of Florida into East and West regions, and Spaniards, Americans, and escaped slaves quickly migrated into the new Spanish Florida, lured by land grants, which were easy to obtain. But instead of becoming a Spanish territory, Florida became

tal seats of East and West Florida. He was one of many politicians who in great earnest tried to tame the turbulent Florida frontier.

The Seminole Indians in Florida History

Over the last two centuries, the Seminole Indians have remained an important part of Florida history. More than any one cultural group, the Seminoles helped shape the political landscape of Florida during the Territorial period. Because of their important contributions to the development of the state, the Seminole Indians are generally believed to be the "native" Indians of Florida. In truth, the origins of this Native American group lie outside of the state, with their roots represented by many different cultural groups from several regions in the southeastern United States.

The Seminoles became Floridians in the 18th century when they began to move into areas once occupied by large groups of indigenous peoples such as the Timucua and the Apalachee. These original native groups were virtually extinct by the early 1700s due to epidemics and extreme cultural, social, and political pressures following European contact around 1500. The resulting voids created by the extinction of these aboriginal groups were filled by Indians who would later become known as Florida's Seminole Indians.

The Florida Seminoles are actually a cultural conglomeration of many groups of Indians, including the Yamasee, driven from the Carolinas

Billy Bowlegs, Seminole Indian leader. Harper's Weekly, June 12, 1858. Engraving made from photograph by Clark, New Orleans.

in 1717, in the Hitchiti-speaking Oconee from the Apalachicola River region, all of which were fleeing an increased presence of colonial whites. Later, they were joined by remnants of the Creek Confederacy from Georgia and Alabama that was defeated in 1814 by General Andrew Jackson at the Battle of Horseshoe Bend. These displaced groups banded together and resettled in northern and north-central Florida.

The Seminoles Indians absorbed the scattered survivors of Native American populations original to Florida as well, including the Timucua and the Calusa. Also, a large number of runaway slaves joined forces with the Seminoles. Many of these slaves had been captured from fierce African warring tribes such as the Ibo and the Ashanti from the Gold Coast. The Seminoles welcomed these capable warriors and permitted them to form their own "Seminole" towns.

The displaced Native Americans from Georgia and Alabama were first referred to as the Seminoles or Siminoles during the late 18th century. The name is a corruption of the Spanish word, "cimarrones," which refers to anything that is wild or untamed. The Spanish used this term to describe the new Indian migrants who left the security of their northern villages to settle the unoccupied Florida interior. Because the Native Americans had no sound relating to the English "r," they pronounced the name "Simalones," which later became "Seminoles." The new name gave timely recognition to a new Florida cultural entity.

There were many Seminole conflicts during

New World Maps

FROM THE COLLECTION OF
THE MUSEUM OF ARTS AND SCIENCES

Catalogue Annotations by
PETER A. COWDREY, JR.

1. Sebastian Münster (1489-1552)   Basle
MAP OF *NOVAE INSVLAE*
From Sebastian Münster, *Geographia Universalis,* 1540
Hand-colored wood engraving
Gift of Kenneth Worcester Dow and Mary Mohan Dow
91.01.545
Image size: 362 x 280 mm.

This was the first printed map treating the western hemisphere as a whole, placing it in the center of the map between Europe and Africa on the east and Asia on the west. It showed the Americas as distinct continents, joined to each other by an isthmus.[1] The Florida peninsula is clearly delineated as the appendage extending south from the land labeled "Terra florida," above Cuba, the island marked "CVBA."

Sebastian Münster was enormously popular, and his Cosmographia, based on the earlier Geographia Universalis, including various forms of his "NOVAE INSVLAE" map, went through numerous German, Latin, French, English, and Czech editions.[2] Sixteenth-century Europeans were very much aware that their world was expanding, and there was intense interest in the reports of explorers returning from far away places.

Although Münster called the American continents "NOVAE INSVLAE," or "New Islands," they were new only to the Europeans who were just then encountering them. The Americas were not new to the Native American peoples who had long occupied them from extreme northern Canada south to Tierra del Fuego.

The map is written in Latin, except for the German inscription across South America that reads, "Die Nüw Welt," or "The New World." The Strait of Magellan is shown below South America, and a ship representing the Victoria, the only one of Magellan's ships to survive the circumnavigation of 1519-22, is depicted in the Pacific Ocean. Above it and to the viewer's left, Marco Polo's 7,448 islands in the northern Pacific are illustrated.

The American continents themselves are depicted as separate from Asia, a fact that would not become known until after Vitus Bering's explorations of northeast Russia in 1728.[3] In this respect, Münster's map is well ahead of its time. On the other hand, Japan, labeled "Zipangú," is placed just to the west of Mexico, and the Yucatán peninsula is depicted as the island of "Iucatana" just east of Mexico.

Most of the labels relating to the Americas are concerned with South America, outlined in yellow, and named "Nouus orbis," or "The New World." Just below this name is the inscription, " Noua Insula Atlantica quam uocant Brasilii & Americam," or "The new Atlantic Island which they call Brazil and America." Present-day Argentina is labeled "Regio Gigantum," or "Region of Giants," and cannibals are shown as occupying Brazil. Extreme northern South America bears a legend declaring that this area labeled Parias, "abounds in gold and pearls."

This reference to vast wealth serves as a reminder that the Spanish conquest was occurring in full force when this map was published. Well before this date, however, the violence of the conquistadores had caused many in the clergy to denounce them and to lobby for laws to protect the Native American peoples. In 1540, the missionary priest Bartolomé de las Casas stood at the forefront of this effort, and he wrote his *Brevísima relación de la destrucción de las indias,* or *A Brief Account of the Destruction of the Indies,* that same year as an indictment of the conquistadores on both continents. Las Casas, Spain's officially appointed Protector of the Indians, would devote the remainder of his life to working on behalf of Native Americans. In the meantime, Hernando de Soto, personifying all that Las Casas opposed, already had begun his entrada into the vast hinterland of Münster's "Terra florida."[4]

Münster's North America is outlined in pink, and it was here that he depicted the greatest geographic inaccuracy of the map. Between what is marked "Terra florida" and "FRANCISCA," Münster included a large area of water known as the Sea of Verrazzano, so named from a feature delineated on a manuscript map of the Italian mapmaker Girolamo da Verrazzano in 1529. Giovanni da Verrazzano, exploring the present-day east coast of the United States for King Francis I of France, apparently confusing the extent of Pamlico Sound and missing the mouth of Chesapeake Bay, believed that he had found the eastern terminus of a great water route to Asia, separated only by a narrow isthmus from the Atlantic Ocean.[6] No such route actually existed, but based on Verrazzano's report it was represented—indeed, it was mapped—as a huge arm of the Pacific Ocean that reached eastward nearly to the Atlantic.

The Sea of Verrazzano found its way onto numerous maps of this period, including Sebastian Münster's "NOVAE INSVLAE." Münster's great popularity helped to perpetuate the myth of this so-called "Northwest Passage," something that would vex European explorers for many years to come.

Notes:
1. Seymour I. Schwartz and Ralph E. Ehrenberg, *The Mapping of America* (New York: Harry N. Abrams, Inc., Publishers, 1980), Plate 18, p. 50.
2. Leo Bagrow, *History of Cartography*, revised and enlarged by R. A. Skelton (Cambridge, Mass.: Harvard University Press, 1964), pp.150-153.
3. Charles Bricker, *Landmarks of Mapmaking: An Illustrated Survey of Maps and Mapmaking,* maps chosen and displayed by Ronald V. Tooley, with a preface by Gerald Roe Crone (New York: Dorset Press, 1989), pp. 130-133.
4. Bartolomé de Las Casas, *Brevísima relacion de la destrucción de las Indias,* translated in 1656

by John Phillips as *The Tears of the Indians,
Being an Historical and True Account of the
Cruel Massacres and Slaughters Committed by
the Spaniards in the Islands of the West Indies,
Mexico Peru, Etc.*, with an historical intro-
duction by Colin Steele (New York: Oriole
Chapbooks, 1972), pp. 56-58. Las Casas'
writings were instrumental in securing
much needed Spanish protection for
Native American peoples, and legislation
such as the Ordenanzas sobre
Descubrimientos of 1573 were a direct
result of his influence. In the hands of the
English and Dutch, however, these same
writings, including the 1656 translation of
John Phillips cited here, were used as anti-
Spanish propaganda, and to lay the founda-
tion for what has been termed the Black
Legend. On this, see Joseph P. Sánchez,
"Hispanic Heritage," in Herman J. Viola
and Carolyn Margolis, eds., *Seeds of
Change: A Quincentennial Commemoration*
(Washington: Smithsonian Institution
Press, 1991), pp. 173-178.

For a recent analysis of de Soto's route
through the Southeast, see Jerald T.
Milanich and Charles Hudson, *Hernando de
Soto and the Indians of Florida*, Riley P.
Bullen Series, Number 13, Jerald T.
Milanich, general editor, Florida Museum
of Natural History (Gainesville:
University Press of Florida/Florida Museum
of Natural History, 1993), *passim*.

5. Lawrence C. Wroth, *The Voyages of
Giovanni da Verrazzano, 1524-1528* (New
Haven, Conn; Published for the Pierpont
Morgan Library by Yale University Press,
1970), pp.191-192, Plate 19, and Plate 22.

6. Carl Moreland and David Bannister,
Christie's Collectors Guides: Antique Maps,
second edition (Oxford, U.K.: Phaidon,
Christie's Limited, 1986), pp. 56-57. See
also Charles Bricker, p. 214.

1. Sebastian Münster (1489-1552) Basle, **Map of *NOVAE INSVLAE***, *From Sebastian Münster,* Geographia
Universalis, *1540.*

2. Tolomeo (Giacomo Gastaldi) (c. 1500-1566)   Venice
MAP, *NVEVA HISPANIA TABVLA NOVA*
From Tolomeo [Giacomo Gastaldi], *Geografia*,
Edited by Girolamo Ruscelli, 1561
Hand-colored engraving
Gift of Kenneth Worcester Dow and Mary Mohan Dow
91.01.460
Image size: 268 x 197 mm.

Tolomeo (also rendered Ptolemeo) is the Italian form of the name, Ptolemy, a mapmaker who lived in Alexandria, Egypt, in the second century, A.D., and who followed the pattern of several earlier Greek geographers in describing places with regard to latitude and longitude.[1] Ptolemy's *Geographia* was translated from Greek to Latin by the Italian Humanist Jacopo d'Angelo more than 1,000 years later, in 1406. Jacopo named the translation *Cosmographia*, the name by which it became most commonly known.[2]

Ptolemy's writings exerted a profound influence on scholars of the Renaissance, and also on the explorers who were sailing to new places all over the globe. Ptolemy himself had described the world as he knew it, from Ethiopia in the south to perhaps Iceland in the north, and from the Canary Islands in the west to possibly China in the east. As reports began to circulate in Europe on the extent of Africa, and regarding the continents of North and South America, some scholars, among them the Venetian Giacomo Gastaldi, simply added the new information to what already was known in Ptolemy.

Ptolemy's greatest cartographic inaccuracy concerns the size of the Earth. In this regard, Ptolemy had endorsed the smaller estimate of Posidonius over the larger one of Eratosthenes. One result of this was that Christopher Columbus believed, following Ptolemy, that the world was considerably smaller than it actually is. [3] This fact helps to explain why he used the term "Indians" to describe the Native Americans of the Lucayos, or Bahama Islands. Not until Magellan's voyage of 1519-22 would Europeans understand the true size of the world. By then, the name "Ptolemy" had become synonymous with collections of world maps and charts and it continued to be used by Gastaldi and others.

Giacomo Gastaldi, Italy's greatest cartographer, published "NVEVA HISPANIA TABVLA NOVA" as an entry in his *Geografia* in 1548. Later editions, including the one from which this map is taken, were published by Girolamo Ruscelli. Ruscelli enlarged Gastaldi's maps and updated several, including this one. Originally this map had depicted Yucatán as an island, but was corrected by Ruscelli to show it as a peninsula.[4]

Mexico's coastal geography and rivers are given in very basic terms, and only a few of its best known cities, such as Mexico City, are identified. The Florida peninsula lies well to the east, attached to the mainland by a narrow isthmus.

The fact that Florida is included on the map is appropriate, for already the annual voyages from Vera Cruz to Havana and on to Spain were a regular feature of Spanish commerce. These voyages brought the homebound Spanish fleets into Florida waters in three broad areas: along the west coast, close to the Keys, and northward along the east coast.

The languages on the map are Spanish and Latin, and its title is translated "A New Map of New Spain." The Tropic of Cancer is shown correctly as passing between Florida and Cuba, and the Pacific Ocean is depicted as the "MAR DEL SVR," or "South Sea." The latitudes given are reasonably accurate, and longitudes are depicted as progressing eastward, presumably from the Canary Islands.

On the Pacific side of Mexico, Baja California correctly is shown as a peninsula. There is considerable detail for the Gulf of California, the Colorado River, and several coastal features of the lower Mexican west coast and present-day Central America.

Notes:

1. Ronald V. Tooley, *Tooley's Dictionary of Mapmakers*, preface by Helen Wallis (New York: Alan R. Liss, Inc., 1979) p. 521. See also Leo Bagrow, *History of Cartography*, Revised and enlarged by R.A. Skelton (Cambridge, Mass.: Harvard University Press, 1964), pp. 34-37.

2. Claudii Ptolemaei, *Cosmographia Tabulae. Cosmography: Maps from Ptolemy's Geography*, translated by Simon Knight, Introduction by Lelio Pagani (Leicester, U.K.: Magna Books, 1990), pp. III-VIII.

3. Charles Bricker, *Landmarks of Mapmaking: An Illustrated Survey of Maps and Mapmaking*, maps chosen and displayed by Ronald V. Tooley, with a preface by Gerald Roe Crone (New York: Dorset Press, 1989), pp. 12-20 .

4. Robert W. Karrow Jr., *Mapmakers of the Sixteenth Century and Their Maps: Bio-Bibliographies of the Cartographers of Abraham Ortelius, 1570*, based on Leo Bagrow's A. *Ortelii Catalogus Cartographorum* (Chicago: Published for the Newberry Press by Speculum Orbis Press, 1993), pp 220-223.

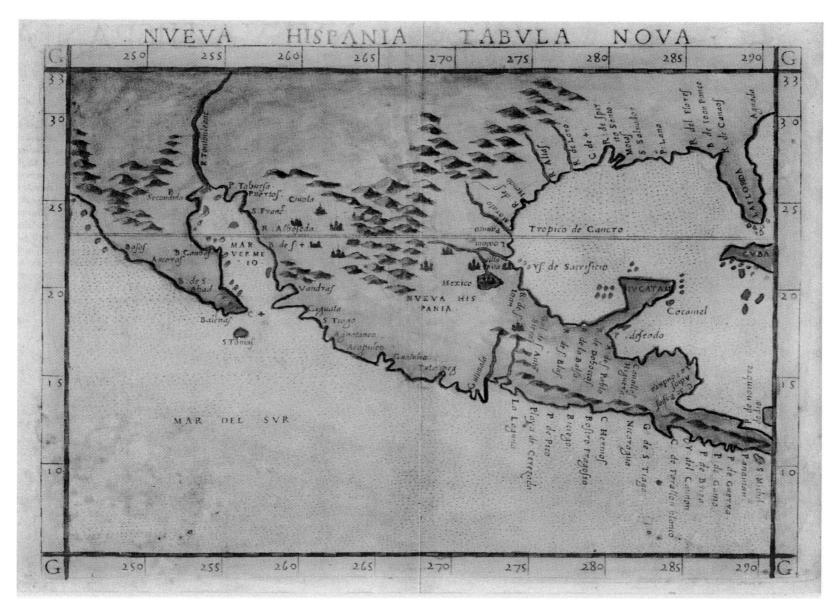

2. *Tolomeo [Giacomo Gastaldi] (c.1500-1566) Venice,* **MAP, NVEVA HISPANIA** *TABVLA NOVA, From Tolomeo, Geografia, 1561.*

3. Abraham Ortelius (1527-1598)   Antwerp
MAP OF *LA FLORIDA*
From Abraham Ortelius, *Additamentum to the*
    ***Theatrum Orbis Terrarum*, 1584**
Hand-colored engraving
Gift of Kenneth Worcester Dow and Mary Mohan Dow
1991
Image size: La Florida, 225 x 152 mm.

Abraham Ortelius, Geographer by special appointment of Philip II of Spain in 1575, was one of the greatest cartographers of his age. He provided the world with its first modern, standardized, printed world atlas, published in 1570. This work, entitled *Theatrum Orbis Terrarum*, ushered in an age of increased geographic precision in printed and bound maps for which there was much demand.[1]

In the years following 1570, Ortelius kept his readers abreast of geographic discoveries by providing them with periodic updates. The two maps here were included in the third such supplement, or *Additamentum*, as it was called, to the original *Theatrum Orbis Terrarum*. This *Additamentum* was published in 1584, and "LA FLORIDA" marks the first known printing of a map of a North American region.[2]

According to the cartouche, the ornate box of information at the bottom of the map, the cartographer of the map is "Hieron. Chiaves," a Latin abbreviation of the Spanish name Geronimo Chaves, who served in the important position of *Piloto Mayor*, or Pilot-Major, beginning in 1552. The second cartouche, in the upper right, bears the inscription, "Cum Priuilegio," or "With Permission" (to publish).

There is no compass rose to indicate directions, but these are provided in Latin near the map borders themselves. North is listed as "SEPTEMTRIO." Elsewhere, "Oriens" is east, "Occidens" is west, and "Meridies" is south. The line marked "Circulus Cancri" at the bottom of the "LA FLORIDA" map is the Tropic of Cancer.

The Spanish claim on La Florida extended considerably beyond the scope of this map, but the major attention here is focused on that portion that was penetrated by Hernando de Soto and his entourage as they fought their way through this region between 1539 and 1543. The map itself is based largely on a c.1544 map ascribed to Alonso de Santa Cruz, and it delineates much of the same topographical information derived from the de Soto march in Florida. Yet, as Cumming has pointed out, there are several important differences between the two maps.[3]

The rectangular shape of the Florida peninsula bears several names in Spanish that are, in Spanish or English, still in use today: C. de Cañaveral (Cape Canaveral), Tortugas (the Dry Tortugas), Rio de pas (Peace River) and Baya de S. Ioseph (St. Joseph Bay).

There is confusion regarding the topography north of present-day Florida, especially with respect to rivers, many of which are shown to intersect, and mountains, which are incorrectly oriented. Longitudes given are unconventional, and may be due to copying errors. There is no mention of St. Augustine, San Mateo, Santa Elena or any of the Spanish missions or coastal forts, perhaps for reasons of security.[4]

According to research undertaken by Cecile-Marie Sastre of Florida State University, the feature labeled "Baya de Baxos" at present-day Apalachee Bay is best translated "Bay of Sandbars," and the place in southern Florida marked "Aguada" may have derived its name as a "Watering Place" for ships.[5]

The map "LA FLORIDA" is accompanied by the map "GVASTECAN," not shown here. It is a continuation of the "LA FLORIDA" map, and begins at the Rio de las Palmas (Palm River) on the Mexican Gulf coast, where the Florida map ends. It follows Mexico southward past Tampico to the "Insula Luporum," or, as it is known today, the Isla de Lobos (Island of Wolves).

A Latin inscription on the "GVASTECAN" map indicates that the prime meridian for this map was Toledo, Spain. When compared to longitudes based on today's Prime Meridian at Greenwich, this map bears strikingly accurate longitudes. This precision extends also to the latitudes, which are very good for both of Ortelius' maps.

Notes:
1. Ronald V. Tooley, *Maps and Map-Makers*, seventh edition (New York: Dorset Press, 1987), pp. 29-30.
2. William P. Cumming, *The Southeast in Early Maps, with an Annotated Check List of Printed and Manuscript Regional and Local Maps of Southeastern North America during the Colonial Period* (Princeton, N.J.: Princeton University Press, 1958), pp. 116-117. See also Ronald V. Tooley, Tooley's Dictionary of Mapmakers, preface by Helen Wallis (New York: Alan R. Liss, Inc., 1979), p. 114.
3. Cumming, *The Southeast in Early Maps*, pp. 116-117.
4. For a fuller discussion of security as it relates to Spanish maps, see "FLORIDA et APALCHE," p. 32 this catalogue.
5. Sastre to Cowdrey, 8 June 1993.

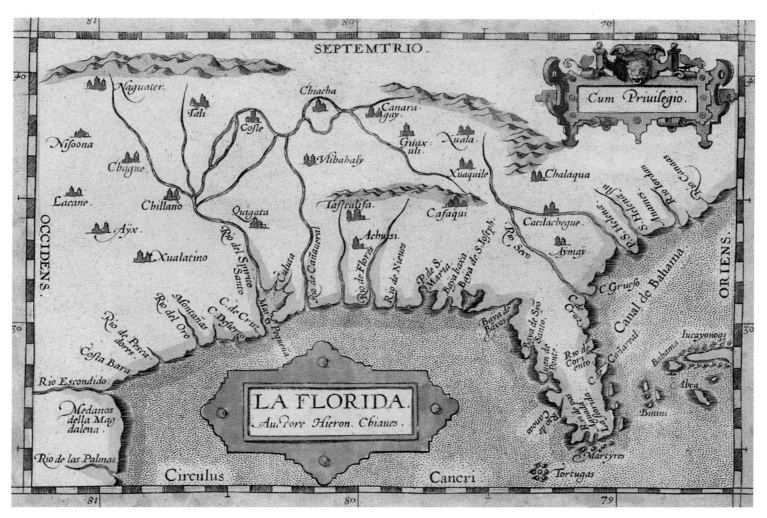

3. Abraham Ortelius (1527-1598) Antwerp, **MAP** OF **LA FLORIDA,** *From Abraham Ortelius,* Additamentum to the Theatrum Orbis Terrarum, *1584.*

4. Gerard Mercator (1512-1594); Jodocus Hondius (1563-1612) Amsterdam

MAP OF *VIRGINIAE* ITEM ET *FLORIDAE*
From Gerard Mercator and Judocus Hondius, *Atlas sive Cosmographicae Meditationes de Fabrica Mundi et Fabricati Figura,* 1606
Hand-colored engraving
Gift of Kenneth Worcester Dow and Mary Mohan Dow
93.04.063
Image size: 505 x 365 mm

Gerard Mercator is the best-known cartographer of the 16th century. Much of his fame rests on his 1569 world map, drawn on a projection known as isogonic cylindrical, later named "Mercator" in his honor. This projection was a great benefit to navigators all over the world because it took the Earth's curvature into account, enabling them to plot accurate straight-line courses to their destinations. Mercator projection still is very much used today.

Late in his life, Mercator conceived the idea of publishing his large *Atlas,* but he experienced several delays in the process. Finally, in 1585 he went to press, but by then the enterprise was so large that his *Atlas* had to be published in stages. He died in 1594 before he could complete its publication, and after his death his map plates were acquired by Jodocus Hondius. Hondius added significantly to it and published their combined work in his *Atlas* of 1606.[1]

The map from that *Atlas* entitled, "VIRGINIAE Item et FLORIDIAE Americae Provinciarum, nova DESCRIPTIO" is Latin for "A New Description of Virginia and Also of Florida, of the Provinces of America." It is inscribed in Latin, but also has French, Spanish and English labels.

The map itself is derived from two earlier maps of the region: the Florida map of Jacques le Moyne, French Huguenot mapmaker and artist at Fort Caroline, 1564-65; and the Atlantic coast map of c.1585 by John White, English veteran of the attempted settlement at Roanoke Island in present-day North Carolina.[2]

The map is a beautiful example of the cartographic skill emanating from the Low Countries in the opening years of the 17th century. Its highly ornate cartouches are attractive as well as informative. The cartouche at the upper left of the map is supplemented with two circular illustrations, one showing a typical Florida Indian town with round houses, the other depicting a Carolina Indian settlement with its oblong lodges. The car-

touche on the lower right declares that the meridians of this map converge in the northern latitudes, indicating that it is drawn on a conic projection.

The elaborate compass rose to the left of the lower cartouche is provided as an aid to navigators. It is marked with a fleur-de-lis for north, and radiates all 32 compass points outward to the coast and to the map borders. In addition, ships are shown sailing in waters inhabited by several varieties of sea creatures.

There are two vignettes on the map. Beside the compass rose is an illustration depicting how the Florida Indians make boats by burning tree trunks, with the observation that in Virginia they do likewise. Near the left border is a second illustration, this one of an Indian king and queen of Florida.

The interior below the main cartouche is meant to be a representation of Florida. One can trace the "R de May," the "River of May," or the present-day St. Johns River inward from the coast to a "Lake so large that from one side, one cannot see the other side," most likely a reference to Lake George.

Geographically, the placement of the Appalachian Mountains in Florida is incorrect, as is the location of the "Lacus et Insula Serrope," possibly a reference to Lake Okeechobee. The east-west trend of the coastline is exaggerated, and St. Augustine is placed too far south.

The interior Florida geography is very detailed with Indian settlements rendered in Timucuan names. Above "S. Augustino," the names of several rivers are rendered in French dating back to the time of Jean Ribault: the Somme, Loyre, Charente, Gironde, Belle, and Grande. At the mouth of the "R de May" near the location of old Fort Caroline is the designation, "Borne de François," or "Limit of the French," referring to the French claim on this part of Florida. Farther north, "Port Royal" is labeled, and just to the east, Charlefort is referenced. For well over a century, French maps of this region would continue to memorialize both Fort Caroline in present-day Florida, and Charlefort in modern-day South Carolina.

Ever since the expedition of Hernando de Soto, European minds had associated the Appalachian Mountains with wealth. Le Moyne's map helped to perpetuate this association. So also did the Mercator-Hondius map, which depicts the "gold-bearing Appalachians," a "lake where Indians find grains of silver," and several Indian towns each having its own "rich king." More than two centuries later, similar reports of gold in the Appalachian Mountains would haunt the Cherokee Indians, and its discovery would drive them from their land.

4. *Gerard Mercator (1512-1594); Jodocus Hondius (1563-1612) Amsterdam,* **Map of VIRGINIAE Item et FLORIDAE,** *From Gerard Mercator and Judocus Hondius,* Atlas sive Cosmographicae Meditationes de Fabrica Mundi et Fabricati Figura, *1606.*

Notes:

1. Ronald V. Tooley, *Maps and Map-Makers,* seventh edition (New York: Dorset Press, 1987), pp. 29-30. See also Leo Bagrow, *History of Cartography,* revised and enlarged by R.A. Skelton (Cambridge, Mass.: Harvard University Press, 1964), pp.179-180.

2. Woodbury Lowery, *The Lowery Collection: A Descriptive List of Maps of the Spanish Possessions within the Present Limits of the United States, 1502-1820,* edited with notes by Philip Lee Phillips (Washington: Government Printing Office, 1912), p .115.

5. Cornelius Wytfliet (d. 1597) Louvain
MAP OF *FLORIDA* ET *APALCHE*
From Cornelius Wytfliet, *Descriptionis Ptolemeicae Avgmentum*, 1598
Engraving
Gift of Kenneth Worcester Dow and Mary Mohan Dow
91.01.542
Image size: 287 x 230 mm

Cornelius Wytfliet's 1598 atlas, *Descriptionis Ptolemeicae Avgmentum*, indicates great interest among European readers for geographic information on the Americas as the 17th century was about to dawn, since the New World was the work's sole focus. For this reason it has come to be known as the first American atlas.[1]

Wytfliet's "FLORIDA et APALCHE" is based largely on the 1584 Ortelius-Chaves map, "LA FLORIDA," but adds considerable scope and detail over the earlier map.[2] It is larger than its predecessor, and includes eastern Mexico, northern Yucatán, northern Cuba, and most of the Bahama Islands.

In several other substantial ways, the 1597 Wytfliet map improves on its 1584 ancestor: the latitude and longitude scales in the borders are divided into even degrees, not given in odd fractions; the longitudes follow a conventional progression; greater detail characterizes the coastline; and there is a greater north-south trend to the Appalachian Mountains west of the area he has labeled "Apalche" — all of this in contrast to the Ortelius-Chaves map of 1584.

Regarding the interior, some of the inaccuracies of the earlier map are repeated here, such as the radiating river patterns. Also, Wytfliet follows Ortelius and Chaves in depicting the Florida peninsula as generally rectangular in shape, and as having a pronounced isthmus where it joins the mainland.

By 1597, the Spanish had a much better understanding of Florida's geography than this map indicates. Under Governor Pedro Menéndez de Avilés, for instance, Spanish expeditions up the St. Johns River and along the Atlantic and Gulf coasts, and those sent overland under Juan Pardo deep into the interior, had yielded much geographic knowledge of Florida. They had not found the Northwest Passage, and they could not locate the sought-after cross-peninsular waterway, but their search for these features did yield a greatly improved geographic understanding of much of the present-day Southeast.[3] These same excursions also had revealed much about the extent and cultural diversity of the Native American peoples of this vast region.[4]

The fact that there were so few published Spanish maps of the Americas in the 16th century is a reflection of Spain's policy of official secrecy with regard to its *padrón reál*, later called the *padrón generál*, or master world chart, and the close supervision of Spanish navigators by the *Piloto Mayor*, or Pilot-Major.[5] The Spanish Crown was opposed to sharing updated geographic knowledge with nations it regarded as potential rivals. Piracy already was a scourge to Spanish commerce, and English and French freebooters were growing ever bolder by the mid-16th century.

Attacks on Spanish settlements in the Caribbean were perpetrated by French mutineers from Fort Caroline in 1564 and 1565. These incidents not only alerted Spanish authorities to the existence of a hostile French base in Florida, but also underscored the dangerous vulnerability to attack of isolated Spanish coastal settlements. Drake's later systematic plundering of the Caribbean and St. Augustine would see those dangers fully realized.

In the meantime, Menéndez had acted with dispatch to end the French presence in Florida. His violent capture of Fort Caroline and his slaughters of French Huguenots near present-day Matanzas Inlet had indeed removed the French threat adjacent to the Spanish shipping lanes, but these events had earned Menéndez undying enmity abroad. Furthermore, they were but the first instances of continued European contention for control of the present-day Southeast. The very survival of Spanish Florida would be tested in the years ahead by a whole assortment of enemies, many of whom would commit atrocities of their own.

Throughout his explorations of La Florida, Menéndez urged a policy of secrecy.[6] Other nations, however, quite willingly portrayed the geography of Spanish America, Florida included. The 17th century saw the production of maps showing settlements along the Spanish Main, the port cities of Nueva España, and isolated outposts in Spanish Florida. In still later years, some of these maps would bear even the the itineraries and sailing routes of homebound Spanish galleons. Accurate maps were fast being seen by many competing powers as a means of acquiring world empire.

Notes:
1. William P. Cumming, R. A. Skelton, and D. B. Quinn, *The Discovery of North America* (New York: American Heritage Press, 1972), pp. 116-117.
2. Ibid.
3. Eugene Lyon, *The Enterprise of Florida: Pedro Menéndez de Avilés and the Spanish Conquest of 1565-1568* (Gainesville: The University Presses of Florida, 1976), pp. 141-142; 149; 168-169; 176; 179-182; and 204. See also Paul E. Hoffman, *A New Andaluccia and a Way to the Orient: The American Southeast During the Sixteenth Century* (Baton Rouge: Louisiana State University Press, 1990), pp. 231-313
4. Ibid., pp. 117, 129-130, 140, 155, 176-177, 182, 198, 202, and 204.
5. Leo Bagrow, *History of Cartography*, revised and enlarged by R. A. Skelton (Cambridge,

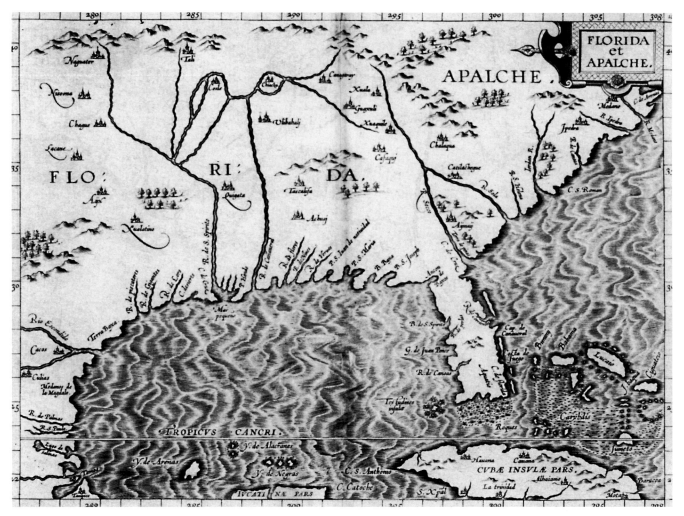

5. *Cornelius Wytfliet (d. 1597) Louvain,* **Map of FLORIDA et APALCHE**, *From Cornelius Wytfliet,* Descriptionis Ptolemeicae Avgmentum, *1598.*

Mass.: Harvard University Press, 1964), pp. 113-115. See also Kenneth Nebenzahl, *Atlas of Columbus and the Great Discoveries* (Chicago: Rand McNally, 1990), p. ix. A contrary opinion on Spanish motives for maintaining tight security on its cartography was offered in the last century by historian Henry Harrisse who argued that Spain wished only to safeguard the integrity of the charts prior to their publication. See Henry Harrisse, *The Discovery of North America: A Critical, Documentary, and Historic Investigation...*, first published in 1892 (Amsterdam: N. Israel, 1969), pp. 257-259.

6. Eugene Lyon, *The Enterprise of Florida*, p. 42.

6. Jan Jansson (d. 1666)   Amsterdam
CHART OF *INSVLAE AMERICANAE*
From Jan Jansson, *Nuevo Atlas*, 1653
Hand-colored engraving
Gift of Kenneth Worcester Dow and Mary Mohan Dow
91.01.555
Image size: 520 x 370 mm.

Jan Jansson's chart of 1653 bears its Latin title in the upper left cartouche: "INSVLAE AMERICANAE IN OCEANO SEPTENTRIONALI, cum Terris adiacentibus," or "American Islands in the Northern Ocean, with Adjacent Lands." Jansson followed in the career of his father-in-law, Jodocus Hondius, and by 1653 already was a renowned maker of atlases, some of them sea atlases.[1]

This is a chart rather than a map, since everything about it indicates maritime application. The loxodromes, or intersecting compass roses and points, radiate across all areas of ocean surface. These are provided as aids to navigation in laying off compass courses. The scale of this chart, however, is too small for practical use, indicating that its most probable use was one of quick reference while at sea rather than for actual navigating.

The scope of the chart is quite large, extending from northern South America to the Chesapeake Bay, and from central Mexico, or "Nova Hispania," eastward past the Lesser Antilles and Bermuda into the Atlantic. The only land areas identified are features of the various coastlines, and its focus is east rather than west, since no part of Mexico's Pacific coast is labeled.

The cartouche in the lower right indicates a comparison of scales between Spanish and German miles, but it actually compares Spanish and German (or Dutch) leagues. Internationally, several nations had their own measures of marine distances, and such scales were needed to provide navigators with their own units. In this case, the Spanish reckoned 17.5 of their leagues to a degree, while the Dutch counted 15 of their leagues in the same distance.

The cherubs on each end of the lower cartouche are holding instruments of navigation dating from the mid-17th century. The one on the left is holding a pair of compass dividers, an essential tool in measuring distances, and the one on the right is lifting a cross-staff, an instrument used in measuring the altitudes of the sun and stars in order to ascertain latitude.

The general appearance of the Florida peninsula is typical of 17th century renditions. There is a marked exaggeration of Cape Canaveral into the Atlantic, and the west coast is overly rounded.

This chart was done nearly 50 years after the English had established Jamestown in present-day Virginia, and less than 20 years before Charles Town (modern Charleston, South Carolina) was founded. Several years after this chart was published, the English occupied the northern portion of the coastal region bounded in green, and Spanish mission towns along the coast in Guale, present-day Georgia, were attacked by English freebooters and driven southward.

The inscriptions in the cartouches are in Latin, and the other nomenclature on the chart is a mixture of several Romance languages. On the peninsula itself, there are two features named "Canaveral": the well-known Cape, and just below it, a feature called "Abra," or "Inlet." Further south is the "Pta S. Luzia," or "Saint Lucy's Point" in the vicinity of modern-day St. Lucie County. Below this is an area marked "Gega," undoubtedly for the Jeaga Indians. The Cape of Florida is well-marked, as are the bays of Juan Ponce, Carlos and Tampa. The upper west coast continues with the Bay of St. Joseph, an "I. del Farellon," or "Point Island," a feature labeled "Gol hondo," or "Deep Gulf," and a river in the northwest peninsula named for the Holy Spirit.

On the east coast above Cape Canaveral a tree is drawn on the coast with the designation, "Boia de Corique," possibly a reference to a mooring place. Above that is the "Barra de mosquitos," or "Mosquito Sandbar," and then a label beside two trees marked, "Arbores de cognoscensa," or "Trees of knowledge," perhaps describing an area of lignum vitae (wood of life) trees.[2] North of that is the "R. de S. Agustin," or "River of St. Augustine." Above that is a "Bay of Saravay," and then the "B. de S. Matheo," or "Bay of St. Matthew," undoubtedly the mouth of the St. Johns River.

Notes:
1. Woodbury Lowery, *The Lowery Collection: A Descriptive List of Maps of the Spanish Possessions within the Present Limits of the United States, 1502-1820*, edited with notes by Philip Lee Phillips (Washington: Government Printing Office, 1912), p.146. This map was based on a 1634 map of Amsterdam cartographer Johannes Blaeu. See Eduard Van Ermen, *The United States in Old Maps and Prints* (Wilmington, Del.: Atomium Books, Inc., 1990), pp. 24-25.
2. This wood was exceedingly valuable and much sought for its supposed medicinal properties, and also for its extreme durability for use in ships' rigging. See Gil Nelson, *The Trees of Florida: A Reference and Field Guide*, drawings by R. Marvin Cook Jr., photographs by the author (Sarasota: Pineapple Press, Inc., 1994), p. 64.

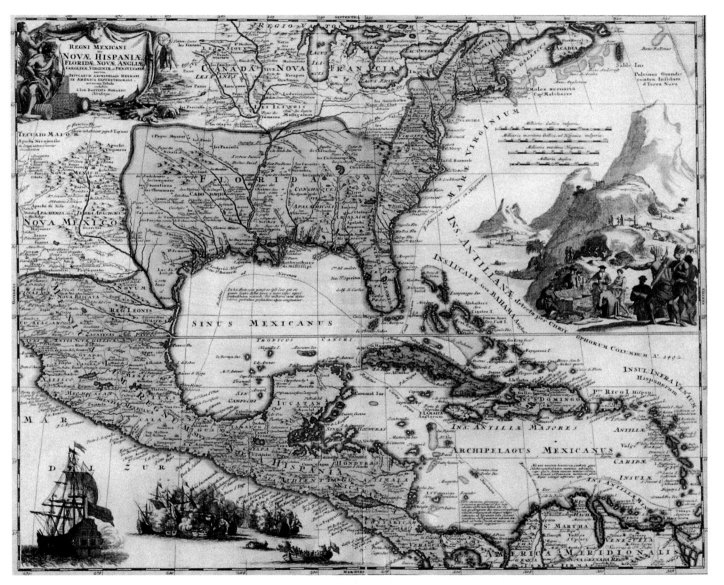

8. *Johann Baptist Homann (1663-1724) Nuremberg,* **MAP OF REGNI MEXICANI SEU NOVAE HISPANIAE**, *From Johann Baptist Homann, c. early 18th century.*

9. Johann Baptist Homann (1663-1724)   Nuremberg
MAP OF AMPLIFFIMAE REGIONIS MISSISSIPI
From Johann Baptist Homann, *Atlas Geographicus Major*
  Norimbergae Homannianis heredibus, 1763
Hand-colored engraving
Gift of Kenneth Worcester Dow and Mary Mohan Dow
91.01.576
Image size: 575 x 486 mm

Johann Baptist Homann brought considerable scientific skill to the profession of cartography, and matched this with a passion for updating his maps in order to keep them current. As Geographer to the Kaiser and member of the Prussian Royal Academy of Science, he was perfectly placed to become Germany's greatest cartographer.[1]

 Homann, of Nuremberg, was the first German map engraver to become a major publisher of large atlases. He was widely regarded as the best German cartographer of his day.[2]

Homann's long title for this map indicates that it was based on the first-hand experiences of the French Franciscan missionary Louis Hennepin, who explored the Mississippi Valley in the 1670s. The cartouche in the upper left includes a likeness of Father Hennepin and depicts Niagara Falls, first documented by that missionary.

A second cartouche in the lower right shows a Native American family, a buffalo, and an egret. Just to the left of this cartouche on the Atlantic coast are several rivers above present-day Florida whose French names are those on the Mercator-Hondius map of 1607: the Somme, Loire, Charente, Garrone, and Gironde.

In fact, Homann's map of Mississippi was taken directly from Guillaume de l'Isle's 1718 "Carte de Louisiane," and uncritically reflected the same French viewpoint of North America that de l'Isle had espoused.[3] The eastern border of the French claim was drawn just as de l'Isle had rendered it, and the French references to their earlier hold on Carolina were copied intact.[4]

The scope of the map is very large, extending from the Tropic of Cancer in the south to the 50th parallel in the north, and from "Nouveau Mexique," or New Mexico in the west to "Nova Anglia," or New England in the east. In short, it encompasses a very large part of what would[8] become the United States.

The Mississippi Valley is well delineated. The great river itself is depicted with two names, the "Mississipi," and the "R. S. Lovis," or St. Louis River, which is shown as originating near the Great Lakes and emptying into the "Golfe du Mexique." Several of its main tributaries are illustrated, including the Missouri,

the Ohio, the "Riviere des anciens Chaoumons" (Cumberland), the "Casquinambaux" (Tennessee), the "Akansas" (Arkansas), and the "Rouge" (Red).

Homann, again following de l'Isle, delineates the geography of Florida with several references to the past. He depicts the de Soto march as a faint line that begins at Tampa Bay and winds its way across much of the Southern landscape.[5] North of the river labeled "S. Jean R.," or St. Johns River, is the designation, "Ancien Fort des Francois," a reference to Fort Caroline. It is placed too far north and on the wrong side of the river, but the inclusion of Fort Caroline, even if somewhat wrongly placed, was a reminder of the former French presence in, and claim on, Florida.

Although this map was published in 1763 by Homann's heirs, it depicts the geographic state of affairs in North America at the conclusion of the War of the Spanish Succession, known in the British colonies as Queen Anne's War (1702 - 13). Earlier French claims on the Mississippi Valley in the 1690s had led to an international race for control of the Gulf coast. Spanish forces reached Pensacola ahead of the French, who went on to occupy both Biloxi Bay and the mouth of the Mississippi. The race was very close, and the French, in turn, arrived just in time to turn back the British. Subsequently, Britain's fears intensified that its colonies were being encircled by hostile powers allied to each other. In the southern colonies, these events set the stage for Queen Anne's War.

The connection of these events to Spanish Florida was very direct. Governor James Moore of South Carolina, sensing war, planned an invasion of St. Augustine. When news of the war reached Carolina in 1702, Moore launched his two-pronged attack southward from Charleston, one going by land, the other by sea. After destroying the Spanish missions of the coast north of St. Augustine,[6] Moore's forces turned their full attention onto the city itself. However, the newly finished fortress, the *Castillo de San Marcos*, withstood the siege, and the Carolinian forces could not breech its walls. Frustrated in this attempt, they looted and burned the city, then retreated to Charleston, taking several hundred captive Indians as slaves.[7]

In 1704, Moore led a second invasion of Spanish Florida, this one directed against the mission district of Apalache in present-day Tallahassee. This attack had disastrous consequences for the mission Indians of Apalache, many of whom were seized by Moore as slaves.[8] Elsewhere in Florida, similar invasions by Carolina Indians allied to the British reached deep into the peninsula in search of other Florida Indians for the Carolina slave markets.

By war's end, the missions were no more, and Spanish Florida lay in ruins. Eventually, its repopulation would come from Indians who, in time, came to be known as Seminoles.[9]

In the meantime, Guillaume de l'Isle's map of 1718 had laid the foundation for extravagant French claims for the interior of North America. In Germany, Johann Baptist Homann's reaction to the de l'Isle map was to copy it virtually intact. On the other hand, Herman Moll, Dutch cartographer in the service of the British, vigorously denounced de l'Isle's claims in a map of his own, published in 1720.[10]

Notes

1. Ronald V. Tooley, *Tooley's Dictionary of Mapmakers*, preface by Helen Wallis (New York: Alan R. Liss, Inc., 1979) p. 308.

2. Leo Bagrow, *History of Cartography*, revised and enlarged by R. A. Skelton (Cambridge, Mass.: Harvard University Press, 1964), p .187.

3. William P. Cumming, *The Southeast in Early Maps, with an Annotated Check List of Printed and Manuscript Regional and Local Maps of Southeastern North America during the Colonial Period* (Princeton, N.J.: Princeton University Press, 1958), pp. 100, 186, and Plate. 47.

4. Compare Homann's map, "Amplissima Regionis MISSISSIPI," with Guillaume de l'Isle's "CARTE DE LA LOUISIANE," illustrated in Pierluigi Portinaro and Franco Knirsch, *The Cartography of North America, 1500-1800* (New York: Facts on File, Inc., 1987), Plate 112, p. 223. The only original contributions in Homann's map appear to be the cartouches.

5. For a comparison of de Soto's route as depicted here with that of recent scholars, see Jerald T. Milanich and Charles Hudson, *Hernando de Soto and the Indians of Florida*, Riley P. Bullen Series, Number 13, Jerald T. Milanich, general editor, Florida Museum of Natural History (Gainesville: University Press of Florida/Florida Museum of Natural History, 1993), Figure 54, pp. 234-235.

6. Glimpses of life in Spanish mission towns along the coast north of St. Augustine were provided by an English survivor of a shipwreck in 1696. In that year, Jonathan Dickinson's ship, the *Reformation*, was wrecked near present-day Jupiter Inlet south of Cape Canaveral. After a difficult journey, the English survivors reached St. Augustine, where they were lodged as guests of the Spanish governor, given food and clothing, and taken north to Charles Town, stopping at missions along the way. Dickinson, an English Quaker, wrote with admiration of the Spanish missions as places of prayer, education, and hospitality. The arrival of the English shipwreck survivors and their Spanish escorts was a major news event in Charles Town in 1696, and Dickinson's book, first published in 1699, became something of an instant colonial best seller. See Jonathan Dickinson, *Jonathan Dickinson's Journal or, God's Protecting Providence...*, edited by Evangeline Walker Andrews and Charles McLean Andrews, with a Foreword and a New Introduction by Leonard W. Labaree (Stuart, Fla.: Printed for Florida Classics Library by Southeastern Printing Company, Inc., 1981), pp. 64-71.

7. Michael V. Gannon, *The Cross in the Sand: The Early Catholic Church in Florida, 1513-1870*, a Discovery Quincentenary Edition, 1492-1992 (Gainesville: A University of Florida Book, University Presses of Florida, 1983), pp 74-75.

8. John Hann, *Apalachee: The Land between the Rivers*, Ripley P. Bullen Monographs in Anthropology and History, Number 7, the Florida State Museum (Gainesville: University of Florida Press/ Florida State Museum, 1988), pp. 264-305.

9. John K. Mahon, *History of the Second Seminole War, 1835-1842*, revised edition (Gainesville: University of Florida Press, 1985), pp. 1-5.

10. See Herman Moll's map, "A New MAP of the North Parts of AMERICA claimed by FRANCE," (page 42).

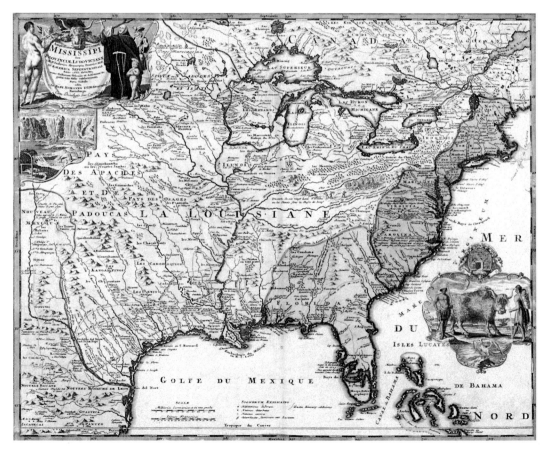

9. *Johann Baptist Homann (1663-1724) Nuremberg,* **MAP OF AMPLISSIMAE REGIONIS MISSISSIPI**, *From Johann Baptist Homann,* Atlas Geographicus Major Norimbergae Homannianis heredibus, *1763.*

10. Herman Moll (fl. 1680-1732)   London
Map, *A New MAP of the North Parts of AMERICA claimed by FRANCE*
From Herman Moll, 1720
Hand-colored engraving
Gift of Kenneth Worcester Dow and Mary Mohan Dow
94.1.281
Image size: 1025 x 615 mm.

Herman Moll was a Dutch cartographer who resided in London, where he published several atlases and maps until well into the 18th century. He was highly regarded for his cartographic skill, and his maps of North America were used by the British government to support British claims in its boundary disputes with France following Queen Anne's War.[1]

In this connection, Herman Moll's 1720 map offers a study in early 18th century diplomatic geography of the American colonies of Britain, France, and Spain, especially when it is compared with a particular map of French cartographer Guillaume de l'Isle. Moll prepared this map with the utmost care regarding threats to colonial British interests occasioned by the geographic claims of the French as contained in de l'Isle's 1718 map of Louisiana.

In the matter of conflicting territorial claims, the cartographer is in a unique position to marshal geographic arguments in order to make them comply with predetermined political and diplomatic goals. In this regard, both Guillaume de l'Isle and Herman Moll were equal to their respective tasks.

The British had two basic objections to the 1718 map of de l'Isle: first, the French mapmaker had pushed the eastern French colonial border too far eastward, just 30 miles west of Philadelphia; second, de l'Isle had argued on his map that English Carolina derived its name from French King Charles IX (it actually was granted by Britain's King Charles II) and that Charles Town was the English name of the former French Charlefort of the 1560s. All of this, plus de l'Isle's use of French names for the area's rivers and coastal features, strongly implied a less-than-subtle French claim on a large portion of the thriving English colony of Carolina.[2]

Moll took the French at their word and illustrated his map of North America with the largest possible French claim as expressed by de l'Isle. It was designed to shock the British public, and to make certain that viewers grasped the fullest understanding of renewed French aspirations in North America, Moll arranged to have the map color-coded. According to his color scheme, French claims in North America, if realized, would leave the British only the area outlined in yellow. By way of contrast, areas outlined in blue would be French and those in red would be Spanish.

Moll had made his point: French claims on the entire trans-Appalachian West would deprive British markets of their Mississippi Valley hinterland, threaten their supply of resources, and keep the frontier in a perpetual state of uncertainty; moving the boundaries eastward would literally squeeze the British settlements east of the Appalachians into a narrow belt along the Atlantic coast; the implied French claim on part of Carolina might even lead to a French effort to detach this section from British control. These claims the British could not and would not allow.

Moll's "Advertisement" lists the genesis of the English claim in North America as stemming from the voyage of John Cabot in 1498, and reminds viewers that the Carolina colony as granted by King Charles II extended westward across the continent "in a direct line to ye South Sea," that is, to the Pacific Ocean. Those guilty of encroachment, argued Moll, were the French.

Regarding Spanish Florida, Moll reasserted the Carolinian claim to the northern portion of the peninsula by giving the southern boundary of Carolina as 29 degrees in conformity with the 1665 provisions of Charles II's Royal Charter This early charter had completely ignored the location of Spanish St. Augustine, placing that city *inside* English Carolina, and granting the English most of the northern Gulf coast. Moll then mapped one of the the slaving expeditions of Carolina's Captain Thomas Nairne. Undertaken during the course of Queen Anne's War, Nairne's raid in search of more Indian slaves had penetrated most of the length of Spanish Florida. Moll's implication was that the British already had virtual control of Spanish Florida, and that eventual British ownership of Florida was a very real possibility.

Notes:
1. Pierluigi Portinaro and Franco Knirsch, *The Cartography of North America, 1500-1800* (New York: Facts on File, Inc., 1987), p. 317. See also Ronald V. Tooley, Tooley's *Dictionary of Mapmakers,* preface by Helen Wallis (New York: Alan R. Liss, Inc., 1979) p. 444.

2. William P. Cumming, *The Southeast in Early Maps, with an Annotated Check List of Printed and Manuscript Regional and Local Maps of Southeastern North America during the Colonial Period* (Princeton, N.J.: Princeton University Press, 1958), pp. 100. See also Verner W. Crane, *The Southern Frontier: 1670-1732,* with a Preface by Peter H. Wood (New York: W. W. Norton & Co., 1981), p. 224-234; and Ronald V. Tooley, *The Mapping of America,* with an index compiled by Douglas Matthews (London: The Holland Press, Ltd., 1985), p. 21. As mentioned above, Homann's map, "Amplissima Regionis MISSISSIPI," contains all of the French claims that the British so deeply opposed.

10. Herman Moll (fl. 1680-1732) London. Map, **A NEW MAP OF THE NORTH PARTS OF AMERICA CLAIMED BY FRANCE***, From Herman Moll, 1720.*

43

11. Jacques Nicolas Bellin (1703-1772)   Paris
PLAN DU PORT DE ST. AUGUSTIN DANS LA FLORIDE
From Jacques Nicholas Bellin, *Petit Atlas Maritime,* 1764
Hand-colored engraving
Gift of Kenneth Worcester Dow and Mary Mohan Dow
91.01.557
Image size: 160 x 207 mm.

This maritime chart of St. Augustine appeared in Volume I of the *Petit Atlas Maritime* of Jacques Nicholas Bellin, the Elder. By virtue of long experience and appointment as Royal French Hydrographer, Bellin was uniquely qualified to make maritime charts.[1] He produced numerous atlases in the course of his professional life, and was a known as a specialist in the waters of the Americas.[2]

Bellin's chart of St. Augustine was published at a time of great transition in Florida, which had changed flags as prescribed in the Treaty of Paris in 1763. The British, having won the Seven Years War or, in the English colonies, the so-called French and Indian War, finally were able to round out their southern colonies with the addition of Florida. Spain, anxious for the return of Havana, which they had lost to the British during the course of the war, traded all of Spanish Florida for the valuable Cuban city.

In a proclamation dated October 7, 1763, the British created two colonies out of the former Spanish Florida: East Florida, extending from the Atlantic to the Apalachicola River, having its capital in St. Augustine; and West Florida, running from the Apalachicola River to the Mississippi River, with its capital in Pensacola.

On reaching St. Augustine July 20, 1763, British Captain John Hedges ordered the Union Jack raised over the *Castillo de San Marcos.* That structure, which had never suffered defeat in open warfare, now became a garrisoned British possession through purely diplomatic channels.[3] Spanish citizens who planned to leave St. Augustine had 18 months to sell their property, if they could find buyers. These Spanish residents of St. Augustine, along with the African-American soldiers and their families from Fort Mose, and remaining Indian groups – virtually the entire population of East Florida –chose to depart in ships for Cuba rather than reside in the new British colony.[4]

Bellin's chart is a simple guide meant to convey ships through the Atlantic breakers between the "Banc du Nord," or "North Bank," and the "Banc du Sud," or "South Bank." Bellin employs the traditional and well-known warnings of shallow water by shading dangerous areas and giving their depths, or soundings. A notation just above and to the left of the fleur-de-lis, or north

arrow, indicates that all depths are given in feet at low water. This is important information since it alerts the pilot and navigator that the soundings are rendered in *pieds*, or feet, and not in *brasses*, or fathoms of six feet each. The lines along the coast further define the hazards of shallow water.

Latitude and longitude are not given on this chart, but a scale of common French leagues is provided in the cartouche at the top. All labels are given in French, and while this is a marine chart rather than a map as such, it does provide a general understanding of the main elements of St. Augustine's geography in 1764. A conspicuous feature is the configuration of the northern end of Anastasia Island, here termed "ISLE DE MATANCE," an obvious reference to the *matanzas*, or slaughters, of Jean Ribault and his followers in 1565 by Pedro Menéndez de Avilés. Also shown are the relationship of "le Fort," that is the *Castillo de San Marcos* to the town of St. Augustine itself; the church of the Indians north of the *Castillo*; and a glimpse of the roads north and west of St. Augustine. The coquina quarry on Anastasia Island is labeled "Cariere," and the coquina watchtower just north of the quarry is given as the "Batise."

Notes:
1. Ronald V. Tooley, *Tooley's Dictionary of Mapmakers,* preface by Helen Wallis (New York: Alan R. Liss, Inc., 1979) p. 49. For a description of Bellin's chart, see Woodbury Lowery, *The Lowery Collection: A Descriptive List of Maps of the Spanish Possessions within the Present Limits of the United States, 1502-1820,* edited with notes by Philip Lee Phillips (Washington: Government Printing Office, 1912), p.337.
2. Pierluigi Portinaro and Franco Knirsch, *The Cartography of North America, 1500-1800* (New York: Facts on File, Inc., 1987), p. 313.
3. Daniel L. Schafer, " '...not so gay a Town in America as this...' 1763-1784," in *The Oldest City: St. Augustine–Saga of Survival,* ed. by Jean Parker Waterbury (St. Augustine: St. Augustine Historical Society, 1983), p. 91.
4. For more on Fort Mose, see Jane Landers, *Fort Mose: Gracia Real de Santa Teresa de Mose–A Free Black Town in Spanish Colonial Florida* (St. Augustine: St. Augustine Historical Society, 1992. Reprinted from *El Escribano* 1991). See also Kathleen Deagan and Darcie MacMahon, *Fort Mose: Colonial America's Black Fortress of Freedom* (Gainesville: University Press of Florida/Florida Museum of Natural History, 1995).

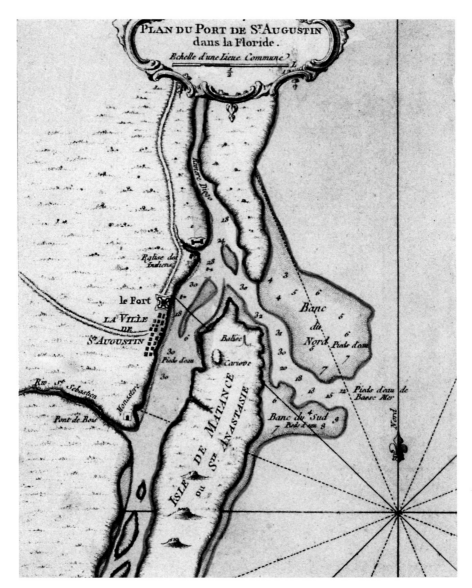

11. *Jacques Nicolas Bellin (1703-1772) Paris,* **PLAN DU PORT DE ST. AUGUSTIN** **DANS LA FLORIDE**, *From Jacques Nicholas Bellin, Petit Atlas Maritime, 1764.*

45

12. Rigobert Bonne (1727-1795) Paris
Map, *L'ISLE DE CUBA*
From Guillaume Raynal, S.J., *Atlas de toutes les parties connues du*
    ***Globe*, Geneva, 1780**
Hand-colored engraving
Gift of Marc Davidson
91.21
Image Size: 343 x 235 mm.

Rigobert Bonne was an internationally known French engineer and cartographer of the late 18th century. Among his widely popular publications were his *Atlas Maritime* and *Atlas Moderne*, 1762, and his two-volume *Atlas Encyclopédique*, 1787-88. Much of his fame rests on the maps he contributed to Guillaume Raynal's *Histoire Philosophique du Commerce des Indies*, 1774, and to Abbé Grenet's *Atlas Portatif*, 1781.[1]

Bonne's 1780 map of Cuba from Raynal's *Atlas* of that year is an excellent depiction of the main topographic features of Cuba. Also, it clearly shows the spatial relationship between Cuba and the Florida Keys just 90 miles across the "DETROIT DE FLORIDE," or Florida Straits.

Irregular lines are shown meandering through the Bahama Islands, above the Florida Keys, and extending southward from Cuba. These lines define the boundaries of shallow water and warn of its hazards.

No compass rose is given, but the map has a fine grid of intersecting lines of latitude and longitude. It is drawn on a plane projection, and provides comparison scales of Spanish and Castilian leagues in the lower left, and common French leagues and French marine leagues in the lower right. The longitudes on the map are given with reference to "L'Isle de Fer," the French name for the "Isla de Hierro" in the Canary Islands.

This map of Cuba delineates the geographic proximity of the two lands, Cuba and Florida, and also serves to symbolize the common links – political, economic, religious, and cultural – that bound the two so closely together throughout the colonial period.

It was these common ties, according to Miguel Bretos, that became the foundation for the continued interaction between Florida and Cuba.[2] This interaction has lasted, and endures still, fueled in recent decades by Castro's rise to power and by the migration of so many Cuban people, seeking refuge, into Florida. Seen in this light, it is no accident that Spanish is spoken widely today in many parts of Florida, that Cuban food is popular in the state's restaurants, or that Florida counts Cuban-born members among its congressional representatives.

The straits that separate Florida and Cuba are represented accurately by Bonne in his map of 1780. These same straits have served as an east-west commercial corridor and as a north-south waterway linking the two neighboring lands for close to 500 years.

Notes:
1. Ronald V. Tooley, *Tooley's Dictionary of Mapmakers,* preface by Helen Wallis (New York: Alan R. Liss, Inc., 1979) p. 69.
2. Miguel A. Bretos, *Cuba & Florida: Exploration of an Hispanic Connection, 1539-1991* (Miami: Historical Association of Southern Florida, 1991), *passim.*

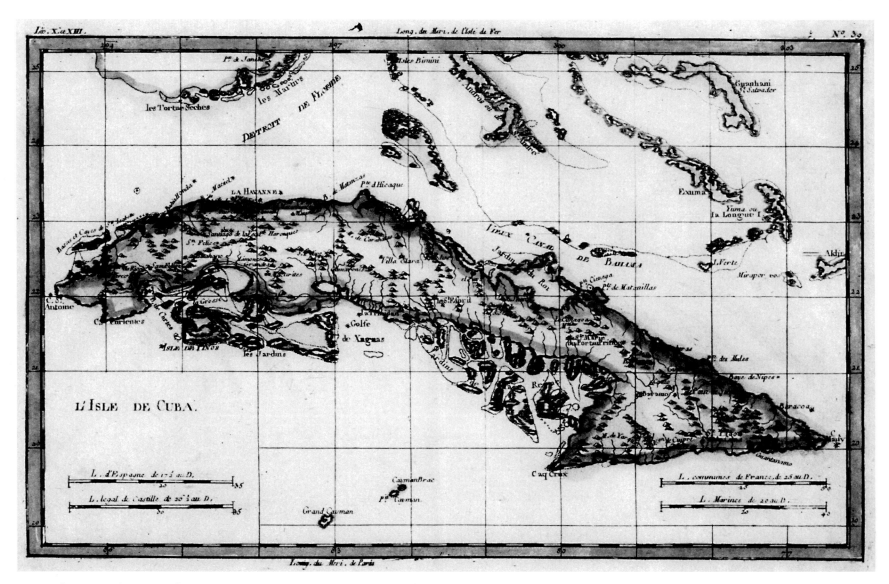

*12. Rigobert Bonne (1727-1795) Paris, **Map, L'ISLE DE CUBA**, From Guillaume Raynal, S.J., Atlas de toutes les parties connues du Globe, Geneva, 1780.*

13. Robert Bénard, (fl. 1750-1785)   Paris
MAP, *CARTE DU GOLFE DU MEXIQUE*
From William Robertson's *l'Histoire de l'Amérique*, 1778
Engraving
Gift of Kenneth Worcester Dow and Mary Mohan Dow
91.01.447
Image size: 476 x 311 mm.

Robert Bénard was a relatively obscure French mapmaker of the late 18th century. He is best remembered for his *Amérique Méridionale*, 1754, and for his French edition of Captain James Cook.[1]

According to information contained in the cartouche, this is a map of the Gulf of Mexico and of the islands and countries adjacent to it, drawn for Dr. William Robertson's *History of America*. The French edition of this work was published in 1778.

Bénard's map of the Gulf of Mexico was made during the American Revolution at a time when the infant United States was fighting for its survival. France, impressed with the American victory over the British at the Battle of Saratoga in 1777, became an American ally. What is perhaps lesser known is that Spain, an ally of France during the recent Seven Years War, also assisted the American war effort.[2]

East and West Florida chose not to join the other 13 colonies north of them, and instead remained loyal to King George III. During the course of the war, Spanish forces under Bernardo de Gálvez harried West Florida, and captured Pensacola from the British in 1781. Two years later, American and French warships fought and won a naval engagement – the so-called Last Battle of the American Revolution – over a British force some 90 miles east of the East Florida coast.[3]

Bénard's map depicts an overly narrow peninsula of Florida with a fragmented and irregular southern portion. This feature was a common one on maps of earlier periods, as Joseph Fitzgerald has shown.[4] Shallow coastal areas are provided with a thin line to seaward indicating the approximate position of the 100-fathom line, marking a depth of 600 feet.

A scale in the lower left compares leagues with English land miles. In the upper and lower borders, longitudes are given as "Ouest de l'Isle de Fer," that is, west from the Canary Island of Hierro. The abbreviated compass rose to the left of the circular cartouche has the familiar fleur-de-lis for north, and a very small but visible cross indicating east. This use of a cross to mark east was a custom already several centuries old originating in the Mediterranean Sea as a means of indicating the direction to the Holy Land. Although this custom was not universally followed, it was commonly used on the maps of many nations, including the charts of the British admiralty, until well into the next century.

Regarding Florida itself, the map compresses the width of the peninsula, rendering it overly narrow. Further, although the two colonies had been separated formally into East and West Florida in 1763, no such differentiation appears on this map of 1778. Also, as noted above, it has the broken islands appearance for southern Florida that is characteristic of maps of the 1760s.

Robert Bénard's 1778 map of the Gulf of Mexico is, compared to other maps of his day, retrograde. British efforts to correct coastlines and undertake very accurate marine surveys of harbors throughout its American colonies had been under way for nearly 15 years, and many of these surveys had been widely published. Bénard's map does not reflect any of this new knowledge.

The British marine surveys taken along the Atlantic and Gulf coasts from 1764 onwards established a new scientific standard for the production of and maps and charts. Competing publishers who did not reflect these new standards stood little chance of success.

The development of the marine chronometer by John Harrison in 1764 had a momentous subsequent influence on navigation, since it enabled navigators for the first time to determine accurately their longitude aboard ship. This in turn led to further refinements in the precision of British marine surveys and in the improved accuracy of British charts.[5] Increasingly, recognition of the excellence of British navigational charts would be expressed in the growing international use of the Greenwich Prime Meridian.

Notes:
1. Ronald V. Tooley, Tooley's *Dictionary of Mapmakers*, preface by Helen Wallis (New York: Alan R. Liss, Inc., 1979) p. 49.

2. For several instances of Spanish support of American aims during the Revolutionary War, see Joseph P. Sánchez, "Hispanic American Heritage," in Herman J. Viola and Carolyn Margolis, eds., *Seeds of Change: A Quincentennial Commemoration* (Washington: Smithsonian Institution Press, 1991), pp. 181-182.

3. House Concurrent Resolution 620 of the 1986 Legislative Session recognized this "Battle Off Florida." See Allen Morris, compiler, *The Florida Handbook, 1993 1994: 24th Biennial Edition* (Tallahassee: The Florida Peninsular Publishing Company, 1993), p. 313.

4. Joseph J. Fitzgerald, Guest Curator, *Changing Perceptions: Mapping the Shape of Florida, 1502-1982* (Miami: Historical Association of Southern Florida, 1984), comments in catalog number 80 (p.79), and in catalog number 83 (p. 79).

5. John D. Ware, *George Gauld: Surveyor and Cartographer of the Gulf Coast*, revised and completed by Robert R. Rea (Gainesville: University Presses of Florida, 1982), pp. 17-21.

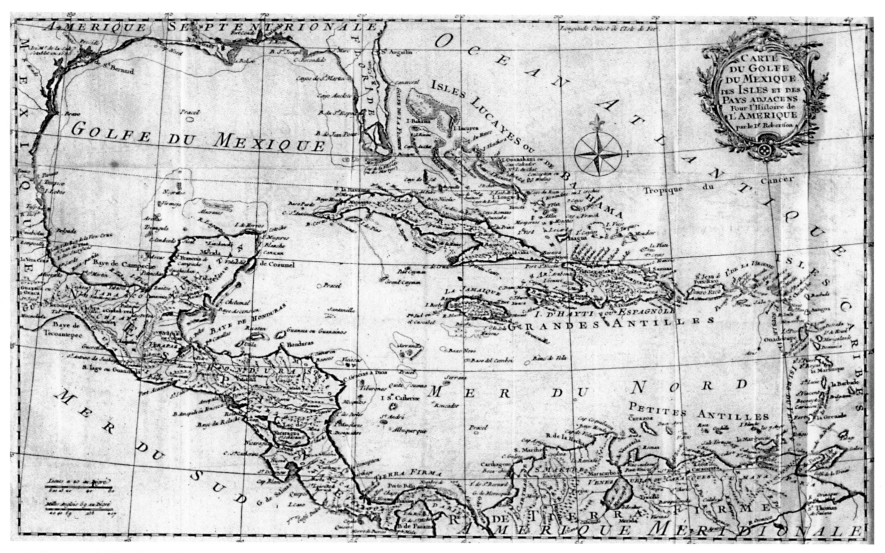

13. Robert Bénard, (fl. 1750-1785) Paris, **Map, CARTE DU GOLFE DU MEXIQUE**, *From William Robertson,* l'Histoire de l'Amérique, 1778.

14. Joseph F. W. Des Barres, 1722-1824   London
Map, A PLAN of the HARBOUR of ST. AUGUSTIN in the
    PROVINCE of GEORGIA
From Joseph F. W. Des Barres, *Atlantic Neptune*, 1780
Engraving
Gift of Kenneth Worcester Dow and Mary Mohan Dow
94.1.280
Image size: 1006 x 765 mm.

Joseph F. W. Des Barres was a British engineer and marine surveyor who surveyed the coasts of British North America for much of his professional life. He also mapped Canadian waters for some years, and his exacting survey methods likely influenced James Cook, future explorer of the South Pacific.[1]

At the conclusion of the Seven Years War in 1763, Great Britain acquired Canada and Florida, and the British Admiralty was very much aware of the inferior nature of the coastal charts of the time. To correct this, the Board of Trade created the General Survey of North America in 1764, and charged it with the responsibility of producing accurate coastal surveys and charts for His Majesty's Dominions in North America, not only for the newly acquired areas, but also for the American colonies as a whole.[2]

The General Survey was an ambitious undertaking, and in order to facilitate mapping, the British colonies were divided into the Northern District and the Southern District, divided by the Potomac River.

Highly scientific British marine surveying methods of the time were applied from Labrador to the Florida Gulf coast with immediate results in improved accuracy. These surveys marked a watershed in the history of British cartography, which now had reached a level of perfection exceeded by no other nation.

The extensive marine survey is what brought George Gauld, Gerard De Brahm, and Bernard Romans to Florida waters in the 1760s and 1770s. During those years, their mapmaking efforts also had drawn the attention of Joseph F. W. Des Barres.

The new charts were made available in publications such as *Collection of Charts*, 1769-70; *North-American Pilot*, 1775; and, Des Barres's *Atlantic Neptune*, 1780. It was the latter publication in which Des Barres's map of St. Augustine first appeared.

According to the map's own identification, it is "A PLAN of the HARBOUR of ST. AUGUSTIN in the PROVINCE of GEORGIA." Of course, Des Barres was mistaken in placing St. Augustine in Georgia. It was, in fact, the capital of East Florida.

That mistake, glaring though it is, is the greatest single criticism of the entire map. Otherwise, it is very good. It is done largely in the style of a marine sailing chart, but includes considerable shore detail. Landmarks, such as the coquina "Light House" on Anastasia Island and "Fort St. Mark," that is, the *Castillo de San Marcos*, are identified.[3]

St. Augustine itself is well mapped, and pertinent water areas are well delineated: the Atlantic approaches between the North Bank and the South Bank; the North River; the Matanzas River; and the St. Sebastian River. Lowland features not visible from the harbor are included, such as agricultural plots of land some distance inland, the defensive wall known as the Mose Wall located two miles north of the city, and "Fort Maze," (i.e., Fort Mose) at the eastern terminus of that wall. Even "Oglethorpe's Battery," the Anastasia Island location from which James Oglethorpe's artillery had bombarded Spanish St. Augustine in 1740, is identified.

Latitudes and longitudes are not given, and compass directions are expressed with regard to true north. Scales are provided for distance computation in feet and statute miles, and soundings are rendered in fathoms taken at high water.

One of the real difficulties experienced in the port of St. Augustine was, as this map shows, its shallow water. In times of naval attack, this worked to the advantage of the city. In times of peace, however, the depth of its harbor would exclude all but smaller vessels. As the years passed, these shallow waters would hamper the growth of St. Augustine, but undoubtedly they contributed to the cultural and architectural preservation the city enjoys today.

Notes:
1. Ronald V. Tooley, *The Mapping of America*, with an index compiled by Douglas Matthews (London: The Holland Press, Ltd., 1985), p. 177.
2. John D. Ware, *George Gauld: Surveyor and Cartographer of the Gulf Coast*, revised and completed by Robert R. Rea (Gainesville: University Presses of Florida, 1982), p. 14.
3. The feature that Des Barres labeled "Light House" probably remained a watchtower until 1823-24. See George E. Buker, "The Americanization of St. Augustine, 1821-1865," in Jean Parker Waterbury, ed., *The Oldest City: St.Augustine – Saga of Survival* (St. Augustine: St. Augustine Historical Society, 1983), p. 153. For more information on the history of this tower, including its possible use as a lighthouse during the British period, see Thomas W. Taylor, *Florida's Territorial Lighthouses, 1821-1845: A Legacy of Concern for the Mariner,* (Allandale, Fla.: A Limited Edition Florida Sesquicentennial Publication, 1995), pp. 16-17.

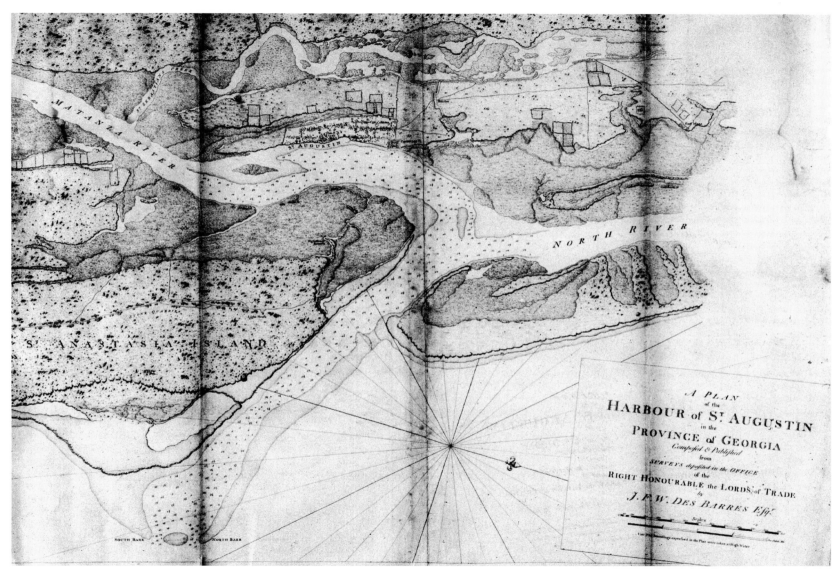

14. Joseph F. W. Des Barres, 1722-1824 London, **MAP, A PLAN** OF THE **HARBOUR** OF **ST. AUGUSTIN** IN THE **PROVINCE** OF **GEORGIA**, *From Joseph F. W. Des Barres,* Atlantic Neptune, *1780.*

51

15. Thomas Jeffreys (c.1710-1771)   London
MAP, *FLORIDA* FROM THE LATEST AUTHORITIES
From William Roberts, *An Account of the First Discovery, and*
    Natural History of Florida, 1763
Engraving
Gift of Kenneth Worcester Dow and Mary Mohan Dow
94.01.446
Image size: 362 x 387 mm

Thomas Jeffreys, Geographer to His Majesty, was a prolific British map-maker of the 18th century. In addition, he knew and understood virtually every aspect of cartography, including surveying, drafting, engraving, and publishing.[1]

This Jeffreys map of Florida first appeared as the frontispiece of William Roberts' *An Account of the First Discovery, and Natural History of Florida*, published in 1763. The Seven Years War, also called the French and Indian War, had just ended, and Great Britain found itself in control of all of eastern North America from the Atlantic Ocean to the Mississippi River.

The map highlights the British colonies of North Carolina, South Carolina, Georgia, and the newly formed East Florida and West Florida. Geographic detail is very sparse for for North Carolina, and is confined to the Atlantic coast where Cape Hatteras, Cape Lookout, and Cape Fear are labeled. For South Carolina and Georgia more geographic detail is provided, especially with regard to the interior. The Appalachian Mountains are shown with relation to the major rivers, and Indian nations are labeled well into the lower Mississippi Valley.

The area labeled "RESERVED LANDS" east of the Mississippi River is a reference to the British Proclamation Line of 1763. This line extended from Lake Erie down the Allegheny Mountains and along the Appalachian crest southward, and later was continued down the Chattahoochee River to its juncture with the Apalachicola. Intended only as a temporary measure, it defined the western limit of colonial settlement until a rational Indian policy could be devised.

However well intended this policy was, it was bitterly denounced by colonists wanting to settle the West, as the trans-Appalachian region was then known. This prohibition on Western settlement continued for years, and became a major grievance of the colonists leading up to the American Revolution.

Meanwhile, East and West Florida were actively encouraging immigration. It was hoped that land-hungry settlers in the 13 colonies to the north could be accommodated in the Floridas. When it became apparent that some West

Florida settlements actually lay north of the 31st parallel, this northern boundary was extended to 32° 28' in order to include them within the colony borders.[2]

According to Jeffreys' own notice in the lower left corner, this map is taken "from the Latest Authorities." It is a synthesis of a number of charts taken from captured French and Spanish ships during the recently concluded Seven Years War.[3] The Florida peninsula is recognizable, but has a very broken appearance characteristic of maps of the 1760s.[4]

Nearly all of the nomenclature for the Florida portion of this map is in Spanish. These designations reflect very powerful Spanish influences exerted on later maps, not only in their use of the name "Florida," but also in the Spanish names of many of its rivers, capes, bays, islands, and keys. Not surprisingly, the names of many of today's Florida counties also are derived from Spanish.[5]

Notes:
1. William P. Cumming, *The Southeast in Early Maps, With an Annotated Check List of Printed and Manuscript Regional and Local Maps of Southeastern North America during the Colonial Period* (Princeton, N.J.: Princeton University Press, 1958), pp. 232-233. See also Woodbury Lowery, *The Lowery Collection: A descriptive List of Maps of the Spanish Possessions within the Present Limits of the United States, 1502-1820*, edited with notes by Philip Lee Phillips (Washington: Government Printing Office, 1912), p. 334.

2. J. Barton Starr, *Tories, Dons, and Rebels: The American Revolution in British West Florida* (Gainesville: University Presses of Florida, 1976), pp. 2-4.

3. Cumming, p. 232.

4. For discussions of a very similar map, see Michael Gannon, *Florida: A Short History* (Gainesville: University Press of Florida, 1993), p. 19. An even more exaggerated French map, that of Jacques Nicolas Bellin of 1764, is offered in Edward A. Fernald and Elizabeth D. Purdom, eds., *Atlas of Florida*, Institute of Science and Public Affairs, Florida State University (Gainesville: University Press of Florida, 1992), p. 83.

5. Allen Morris, compiler, *The Florida Handbook, 1993-1994: 24th Biennial Edition* (Tallahassee: The Florida Peninsular Publishing Company, 1993), pp. 418-434.

15. Thomas Jeffreys (c.1710-1771)   London, **Map, FLORIDA from the Latest Authorities***, From*
William Roberts, An Account of the First Discovery, and Natural History of Florida, *1763.*

16. Joseph Goldsborough Bruff (1804-1889)   Washington, D.C.
MAP, *THE STATE OF FLORIDA*
Compiled in the Bureau of Topographical Engineers (Washington,
    D.C. U.S. War Department... Corps of Engineers) 1846.
Engraving
Gift of Marc Davidson
91.22
Image size: 1030 x 1150 mm.

J. Goldsborough Bruff drew upon the extensive resources of the War Department in the aftermath of the Second Seminole War (1835-42) to produce this map. It was this conflict that underscored the extent of American ignorance with regard to Florida's geography and, paradoxically, provided the incentive for the Army to correct it.

As late as 1837, John Lee Williams of Pensacola published a map of Florida *minus* Lake Okeechobee, whose existence he had not as yet confirmed.[1] On Christmas Day of that very year, Colonel Zachary Taylor's forces met the Seminoles on the shores of that lake in an engagement known to history as the Battle of Okeechobee.[2]

In countless other ways, the nation began to learn of Florida's interior geography only as the war progressed. The course and extent of many of Florida's rivers – the St. Johns, Withlacoochee, Caloosahatchee, and Peace among them – appeared on maps only as a result of military inquiry. The same is true of the interior of the Everglades and the Central Florida lake district.[3]

Bruff's map of Florida was published when all of these memories still were very fresh, just one year after Florida entered the Union as the 27th state. The Second Seminole War was over, and although the military presence still was very obvious in the new state, the map nevertheless reflected the future aspirations of many.

The map is indeed a forward-looking document, and considerable detail is devoted to outlining proposed transportation improvements. The most ambitious of these was the cross-state railroad envisioned in the large inset at the lower left. Fifteen years later this dream would become a reality when on March 1, 1861, the first train of the Florida Railroad would roll into Cedar Key from Fernandina.[4]

A second inset shows the mouth of the Suwannee River and the Cedar Keys with regard to the proposed railroad line. Here again, improvements in transportation and communication would result from these plans. Telegraph lines subsequently linked both sides of the state, and a mail route later connected Cedar Key with Havana.[5]

An important feature of the map is the division of the state into several sections, listed as West Florida, Middle Florida, East Florida, and South Florida. This delineation was consistent with Article V of the Florida Constitution of 1838-39 providing for four circuit courts in the areas named.[6]

The largest national issue facing the United States in 1845 was slavery. It divided the nation early on, and under the terms of the 1820 Missouri Compromise, Florida, a slave state, had been admitted along with Iowa, a free state. In 1845, Florida had a population of 66,381 people residing in 26 counties. Of that number, 30,015, or nearly half, were slaves.[7]

Very conspicuous on the map are the intersecting lines of the Florida Survey, a grid of ranges and townships emanating from Tallahassee. The Second Seminole War had interrupted that survey and still was incomplete when this map was published in 1846. Most of the Seminoles, both Native Americans and African-Americans, had been forced to relocate to the Indian Territories in the West by 1842, but others remained in Florida.

With regard to that survey and to the impact it was likely to have on the surviving Seminoles, there is a note on the map just east of Ostego Bay in southwestern Florida announcing: "20 Miles around this District is reserved from Survey till the Seminoles are removed." Just north, west, and south of this inscription, numerous military forts are depicted: Forts Thompson, Demand (i.e., Deynaud), T.B. Adams, Simmons, Harvey, Dulaney, Duane, Keais, and Foster. In such circumstances, and with the Armed Occupation Act already encouraging homesteading on the Florida frontier, it was only a matter of time before the Third Seminole War would force all but a remnant of Florida Seminoles to move west.[8]

Notes:
1. John Lee Williams, *The Territory of Florida: Or Sketches of the Topography, Civil and Natural History of the Country, the Climate, and the Indian Tribes from the First Discovery to the Present Time*, a facsimile reproduction of the 1837 edition, introduction by Herbert J. Doherty Jr., Floridiana Facsimile & Reprint Series (Gainesville: University of Florida Press, 1962), p. 61 and map endpaper.

2. John K. Mahon, *History of the Second Seminole War, 1835-1842*, revised edition (Gainesville: University of Florida Press, 1985), pp. 227-230.

3. Ibid., p.129 and 249-251. See also "A Map of the Seat of War in Florida 1836" in *American State Papers*, Vol. VII, *Military Affairs* (Washington: Gales and Seaton, 1836). pp. 994-996; and Captain John Mackay, *Map of the Seat of War in Florida …1839* (Washington: W.J. Stone, 1839).

4. Charlton Tebeau, *A History of Florida*, revised edition (Coral Gables: University of Miami, 1985), p. 191.

5. Ibid.

16. *Joseph Goldsborough Bruff (1804-1889) Washington, D.C.,* **MAP, THE STATE OF FLORIDA**, *Compiled in the Bureau of Topographical Engineers (Washington, D. C., U. S. War Department, Corps of Engineers) 1846.*

6. Given in Dorothy Dodd, *Florida Becomes a State*, foreword by W. T. Cash, introduction and edited documents by Dorothy Dodd (Tallahassee: Florida Centennial Commission, 1945), Art. V, Cap. 5, p. 313.

7. Dorothy Dodd, "Florida's Population in 1845," *Florida Historical Quarterly*, vol. 25, no. 1 (July 1945), pp. 28-29.

8. John K. Mahon, *History of the Second Seminole War, 1835-1842*, revised edition (Gainesville: University of Florida Press, 1985) p. 321.

Distant Shores of Foreign Lands

THE NAVIGATOR AS MAPMAKER
IN FLORIDA WATERS

PETER A. COWDREY, JR.

The technology that allowed Spanish explorers to cross strange oceans and make landfall on unfamiliar coasts during the late 15th century was mainly nautical and navigational in character. The Spanish nautical technology was advanced and their ships were fully capable of sustaining long-range, transoceanic voyages.[1] Of equal importance was that the infant science of navigation provided a primitive means for charting voyages through the trackless seas, which in turn enabled the return of these vessels to their home ports.[2]

By the early decades of the 16th century, Spanish navigators, or pilots as they were called, acquired very specialized training under the direction of the newly created *Piloto Mayor,* or Pilot-Major. This training included a working knowledge of navigational theory, meteorology, astronomy, and sailing, and inculcated in trainees a close familiarity with a whole range of officially approved navigational instruments.[3]

The most important navigational device on board the ships of this period was the mariner's compass. This was a dry-mounted circular card, marked on its upper face with 32 points and fitted on its underside with a pointed and magnetized loop. The card was housed in a circular container that was in turn attached by free-swinging gimbals to the inside of a larger box, or binnacle. This design allowed the compass to remain level even during rough weather. The compass was placed so that the helmsman could see it in order to steer his course. At night, it was illuminated by candles.

Time at sea was reckoned in half hours, which were timed by the *ampolleta,* or the sandglass. At each turn of this glass, the helmsman recorded the ship's course and estimated speed on a traverse board. This was a circular board, marked like the compass in 32 points, and having 32 rows with eight holes in each row. These radiated outward from the center. Along the bottom were eight rows with up to 10 holes in each row. Eight pegs were attached by strings to the center of the board, and eight more were suspended from the bottom.

This arrangement enabled the helmsman to record every possible course direction and estimated speed for each half hour of his four-hour watch. After eight turns of the *ampolleta,* the information was taken from the traverse board and written down by the officer in charge. The board was then cleared by the officer for use by the next helmsman.

Each day at noon, weather permitting, the sun's zenith distance was observed using an astrolabe. This was a circular instrument, usually bronze, with a diameter of some six inches, marked on its outer circumference in degrees. It had an alidade, or straight ruler, which pivoted on a pin through the center of the instrument. Near each end of the alidade was a pinule, or small sighting vane, which was pierced with a small hole.

Choosing the moment when the sun was highest in the sky, the

Lowery, Woodbury. *The Lowery Collection: A descriptive List of Maps of the Spanish Possessions within the Present Limits of the United States, 1502-1820.* Edited with notes by Philip Lee Phillips. Washington: Government Printing Office, 1912.

Lyon, Eugene. *The Enterprise of Florida: Pedro Menéndez de Avilés and the Spanish Conquest of 1565-1568.* Gainesville: The University Presses of Florida, 1976.

Mackay, Captain John. *Map of the Seat of War in Florida compiled by order of Bvt. Brigr. Genl. Z. Taylor, principally from the surveys and reconnaissances of the Officers of the U. S. Army, by Capt. John Mackay and Lieut. J. E. Blake U. S. Topographical Engineers, Headquarters, Army of the South, Tampa Bay, Florida, 1839.* Washington: W. J. Stone, 1839.

Mahon, John K. *History of the Second Seminole War, 1835-1842.* Revised edition. Gainesville: University of Florida Press, 1985.

Marx, Robert F. *Shipwrecks in Florida Waters: A Billion Dollar Graveyard.* Chuluota, Fla: The Mickler House, Publishers, 1985.

Medina, Pedro de. *Regimiento de Navegacion....* Seville: Casas de Simon Carpintero, 1563. Reprinted in facsimile. Madrid: Instituto de España, 1964.

Milanich, Jerald T. *Archaeology of Precolumbian Florida.* Gainesville: University Press of Florida, 1994.

Milanich, Jerald T. and Charles Hudson. *Hernando de Soto and the Indians of Florida.* Ripley P. Bullen Series. Number 13. Jerald T. Milanich, general editor. Florida Museum of Natural History. Gainesville: University Press of Florida/Florida Museum of Natural History, 1993.

Milanich, Jerald T. and Nara B. Milanich. "Notes and Documents–Revisiting the Freducci Map: A Description of Juan Ponce DeLeon's 1513 Florida Voyage?" *Florida Historical Quarterly* 74 (Winter 1996): 319-328.

Milanich, Jerald T. and Susan Milbrath, eds. *First Encounters: Spanish Explorations in the Caribbean and the United States, 1492 - 1570.* Gainesville: University Press of Florida, 1989.

Morison, Samuel Eliot. *Admiral of the Ocean Sea: A Life of Christopher Columbus.* Maps by Erwin Raisz. Drawings by Bertram Greene. Boston: Little, Brown and Company, 1942.

_____. *The European Discovery of America: The Northern Voyages, A. D. 500-100.* New York: Oxford University Press, 1971.

_____. *The European Discovery of America: The Southern Voyages, A. D. 1492-1616.* New York: Oxford University Press, 1974.

Morris, Allen, compiler. *The Florida Handbook, 1993-1994: 24th Biennial Edition.* Tallahassee: The Florida Peninsular Publishing Company, 1993.

Moreland, Carl and David Bannister. *Christie's Collectors Guides: Antique Maps.* Second Edition. Oxford, UK: Phaidon, Christie's Limited, 1986.

Nabenzahl, Kenneth. *Atlas of Columbus and the Great Discoveries.* Chicago: Rand McNally, 1990.

Nelson, Gil. *The Trees Of Florida: A Reference and Field Guide.* Drawings by R. Marvin Cook, Jr. Photographs by the author. Sarasota: Pineapple Press, Inc., 1994.

Palacio, Diego Garcia de. *Instrucion Nautica, para el Buen Uso....* Mexico: Casa de Pedro Ocharte, 1587. Translated by J. Bankston. Bisbee, Az: Terrenate Associates, 1986.

Parry, John H. *The Age of Reconnaissance.* New York: A Mentor Book from The New American Library, 1964.

Patrick, Rembert W. and Allen Morris. *Florida Under Five Flags.* Gainesville: University of Florida Press, 1967.

Pigafetta, Antonio. *The Voyage of Magellan: The Journal of Antonio Pigafetta.* Translated by Paula Spurlin Paige. Englewood Cliffs, N.J.: Prentice Hall, 1969.

Portinaro, Pierluigi and Franco Knirsch. *The Cartography of North America, 1500-1800.* New York: Facts on File, Inc., 1987.

Ptolemaei, Claudii. *Cosmographia Tabulae. Cosmography: Maps from Ptolemy's Geography.* Translated by Simon Knight. Introduction by Lelio Pagani. Leicester, U.K.: Magna Books, 1990.

Real y Supremo Consejo de las Indias. *Recopilacion de los Leyes de los Reynos de las Indias ...*Madrid: la Viuda de D. Joaquin Ibarra, Impresora de Dicho Real y Supremo Consejo, 1791. Republished in Madrid by Gráficas Ultra, 1943.

Sánchez, Joseph P. "Hispanic American Heritage." *Seeds of Change: A Quincentennial Commemoration.* Edited by Herman J. Viola and Carolyn Margolis. Washington: Smithsonian Institution Press, 1991.

Sastre, Cecile-Marie. Letter to Peter Cowdrey, 8 June 1993.

Schafer, Daniel L. " '...not so gay a Town as this...': 1763-1784." *The Oldest City: St. Augustine – Saga of Survival.* Edited by Jean Parker Waterbury. St. Augustine: St. Augustine Historical Society, 1983.

Schwartz, Seymour I. and Ralph E. Ehrenberg. *The Mapping of America.* New York: Harry N. Abrams, Inc., Publishers. 1980.

Smith, Roger C. *Vanguard of Empire: Ships of Exploration in the Age of Columbus.* New York: Oxford University Press, 1993.

Starr, J. Barton. *Tories, Dons, and Rebels: The American Revolution in British West Florida.* Gainesville: University

Presses of Florida, 1967.

Taylor, Eva G. R. *The Haven-Finding Art: A History of Navigation from Odysseus to Captain Cook.* Foreword by Commodore K. St. B. Collins, R. N. Appendix by Joseph Needham, F. R. S. New York: American Elsevier Publishing Company, Inc., 1971.

Taylor, Thomas W. *Florida's Territorial Lighthouses, 1821-1845: A Legacy of Concern for the Mariner.* Allandale, Fla.: A Limited Edition Florida Sesquicentennial Publication, 1995.

Tebeau, Charlton. *A History of Florida.* Revised edition. Coral Gables: University of Miami, 1985.

Tooley, Ronald V. *Tooley's Dictionary of Mapmakers.* Preface by Helen Wallis. New York: Alan R. Liss, Inc., 1979

_____. *Maps and Map-Makers.* Seventh edition. New York: Dorset Press, 1987.

_____. *The Mapping of America.* Index compiled by Douglas Matthews. London: The Holland Press, Ltd., 1985.

Waghenar, Lucas Janszoon. *Spieghel der Zeevaerdt....* Brabant: 1584. Translated by Anthony Ashley as *The Mariners Mirrour....* London: 1588. Reprinted in facsimile. Amsterdam: Theatrum Orbis Terrarum, Ltd., 1966.

Ware, John D. *George Gauld: Surveyor and Cartographer of the Gulf Coast.* Revised and completed by Robert R. Rea. Gainesville: University Presses of Florida, 1982.

Waters, David W. *The Art of Navigation in England in Elizabethan and Early Stuart Times.* With a Foreword by Admiral of the Fleet The Earl Mountbatten of Burma. London: Hollis and Carter, 1958.

Weddle, Robert S. *Spanish Sea: The Gulf of Mexico in North American Discovery, 1500-1685.* College Station, Tex.: Texas A&M University Press, 1985.

Wroth, Lawrence C. *The Voyages of Giovanni da Verrazzano, 1524-1528.* New Haven, Conn.: Published for The Pierpont Morgan Library by Yale University Press, 1970.

Williams, John Lee. *The Territory of Florida: Or Sketches of the Topography, Civil and Natural History of the Country, the Climate, and the Indian Tribes from the First Discovery to the Present Time.* A facsimile reproduction of the 1837 edition. Introduction by Herbert J. Doherty, Jr. Floridiana Facsimile & Reprint Series. Gainesville: University of Florida Press, 1962.

Zamorano, Rodrigo. *Compendiode la Arte de Navegar....* Seville: 1581. Reprinted in facsimile. Madrid: Ministerio de Educacion y Ciencia, Direccion General de Archivos y Bibliotecas, Instituto Bibliografico Hispanico, 1973.

DANA STE.CLAIRE IS CURATOR OF HISTORY AND AN
ARCHAEOLOGIST WITH THE MUSEUM OF ARTS AND
SCIENCES, DAYTONA BEACH, FLORIDA.

PETER A. COWDREY, JR. IS A MUSEUM PROGRAM
SUPERVISOR AND EARLY FLORIDA MAP SPECIALIST WITH
THE MUSEUM OF FLORIDA HISTORY, TALLAHASSEE.

I thank all those who assisted me in the preparation of the maps portion of this publication. In particular, I am grateful to the following individuals: Ms. Marianne Donnell, Maps Librarian, Documents/Maps/Micro Materials Department, Strozier Library, Florida State University; John H. Hann, Ph. D., Historian, Bureau of Archaeological Research, Division of Historical Resources, Florida Department of State; Joe Knetsch, Ph.D., Senior Management Analyst II, Bureau of Survey and Mapping, Division of State Lands, Florida Department of Environmental Protection; Mr. Charles R. McNeil, Senior Curator, Museum of Florida History, Division of Historical Resources, Florida Department of State; Mr. Erik Robinson, Historian Curator, Museum of Florida History, Division of Historical Resources, Florida Department of State; Mr. Dana Ste. Claire, Archaeologist and Curator of History, Museum of Arts and Sciences, Daytona Beach, Florida; Ms. Stacey Stivers, Graphics Designer, Museum of Arts and Sciences, Daytona Beach, Florida; and last but by no means least, my wife, Carol, whose support and endless patience are the principal reasons for its completion. To her I dedicate this final result.

Peter A. Cowdrey, Jr.